Lectionary
Advent 2018 to the eve of Advent 2019 (Year C)

Church House Publishing

Published by	Church House Publishing Church House Great Smith Street London SW1P 3AZ
Compilation ©	The Archbishops' Council 2018
ISBN	978-0-7151-2337-9 (standard) 978-0-7151-2338-6 (large)
All rights reserved	No part of this publication may be reproduced in any form or by any means, electronic or mechanical, including photocopying, recording, or any information storage and retrieval system, except as stated below, without written permission which should be sought from the Copyright Administrator, The Archbishops' Council, Church House, Great Smith Street, London SW1P 3AZ Email: copyright@churchofengland.org
Authorization	The Common Worship Calendar and Lectionaries are authorized pursuant to Canon B 2 of the Canons of the Church of England for use until further resolution of the General Synod of the Church of England.
Copyright and Acknowledgements	*The Revised Common Lectionary* is copyright © The Consultation on Common Texts: 1992. The Church of England adaptations to the Principal Service Lectionary are copyright © The Archbishops' Council, as are the Second and Third Service Lectionaries, the Weekday Lectionary for Morning and Evening Prayer and the Additional Weekday Lectionary. The Daily Eucharistic Lectionary derives, with some adaptation, from the *Ordo Lectionum Missae* of the Roman Catholic Church and is reproduced by permission of The International Commission on English in the Liturgy. Edited by Peter Moger Designed by Derek Birdsall & John Morgan/Omnific Typeset by RefineCatch Ltd, Bungay, Suffolk Printed in England by Core Publications Ltd

Contents of this booklet

This booklet gives details of the full range of possibilities envisaged in the liturgical calendar and lectionary of Common Worship. Its use as a tool for the preparation of worship will require the making of several choices based first on the general celebration of the Christian year by the Church of England as a whole; second on the customary pattern of calendar in the diocese, parish and place of worship; and third on the pattern of services locally.

The **first column** comprises the Calendar of the Church with the days of the year. Observances that are mandatory are printed either in **bold** type (Sundays), in **bold** type (Principal Feasts and Holy Days) or in roman (Festivals). Optional celebrations (Lesser Festivals) and Commemorations are printed in ordinary roman type and *italic* type respectively.

The **second column** comprises (a) the readings and psalms for the Principal Service on Sundays, Principal Feasts and Holy Days, and Festivals, and (b) Holy Communion readings and psalms for other days of the week. On the Sundays after Trinity, the Old Testament reading and its psalm are divided into two smaller columns, indicating a choice between a 'continuous' reading week by week or a reading 'related' to the Gospel for that day.

The **third column** comprises (a) the Third Service readings and psalms for Sundays, Principal Feasts and Holy Days, and Festivals, and (b) the readings and psalms for weekday Morning Prayer.

The **fourth column** comprises (a) the Second Service readings and psalms for Sundays, Principal Feasts and Holy Days, and Festivals, and (b) the readings and psalms for weekday Evening Prayer.

An **Additional Weekday Lectionary**, intended particularly for use in places of worship that attract occasional rather than daily worshippers, is provided on pages 67–74. It may be used either at Morning or Evening Prayer.

Common of the Saints

General readings and psalms for saints' days can be found on pages 77–81; for some particular celebrations, other readings are suggested there.

Special Occasions

Readings and psalms for special occasions can be found on pages 82–83.

Liturgical colours

Appropriate liturgical colours are suggested in this booklet. They are not mandatory; traditional or local use may be followed.

Colours are indicated by single letters: the first (always upper case) for the season or Festival; and occasionally a second (lower case) for an optional celebration on that day. Thus, for example, *Gr* for the celebration of a Lesser Festival whose liturgical colour is red, in an otherwise 'green' season.

The following abbreviations are used:

G	Green
P or p	Purple or Violet
P(La)	Purple or Lent array
R or r	Red
W or w	White (Gold is indicated where its use would be appropriate)

Contents of this booklet

Notes on the Lectionary

Sundays, Principal Feasts and Holy Days and Festivals

Three sets of psalms and readings are provided for each Sunday, Principal Feast or Holy Day and Festival.

The **Principal Service lectionary** (based on the Revised Common Lectionary) is intended for use at the principal service of the day (whether this service is Holy Communion or some other authorized form). In most Church communities, this is likely to be the mid-morning service, but the minister is free to decide which service time normally constitutes the Principal Service of the day. This lectionary may be used twice if required – for example, at an early celebration of Holy Communion and then again at a later one.

If only **two readings** are used at the Principal Service and that service is Holy Communion, the second reading must always be the Gospel reading. When the Principal Service lectionary is used at a service other than Holy Communion, the Gospel reading need not always be chosen.

The **Second Service lectionary** is intended for a second main service. In many churches, this lectionary may be the appropriate provision for a Sunday afternoon or evening service. A Gospel reading is always provided so that this lectionary can, if necessary, be used where the second main service is a celebration of Holy Communion.

The **Third Service lectionary**, with shorter readings, is intended where a third set of psalms and readings is needed and is most appropriate for use at an office. A Gospel reading is not always provided, so this lectionary is not suitable for use at Holy Communion.

Weekdays

The Common Worship Weekday Lectionary authorized by the General Synod in 2005 comprises a lectionary (with psalms) for Holy Communion, a lectionary for Morning and Evening Prayer, and tables of psalms for Morning and Evening Prayer.

The **Daily Eucharistic Lectionary** (based on the Roman Catholic daily eucharistic lectionary) is a semi-continuous two-year lectionary with a wide use of scripture, though not complete coverage of the Bible. Two readings are provided for each day, the first from either the Old or New Testament, the second always a Gospel. Psalm provision is intended to be a brief response to the first reading. It is for use at Holy Communion normally in places with a daily or near-daily celebration with a regular congregation. It may also be used as an office lectionary.

The **lectionary for Morning and Evening Prayer** always provides two readings for each office, the first from the Old Testament and the second from the New Testament. These are generally in sequence. One of the New Testament readings for any particular day is from the Gospels.

The **psalms for Morning and Evening Prayer** follow a sequential pattern in Ordinary Time (apart from the period from All Saints to the beginning of Advent).

In the periods from All Saints until 18 December, from the Epiphany until the Presentation of Christ in the Temple (Candlemas), from Ash Wednesday until Palm Sunday, and from the Monday after Easter Week until Pentecost, there is a choice of psalms at Morning and Evening Prayer. The psalms printed first reflect the theme of the season. Alternatively, the psalms from the Ordinary Time cycle may be used. The two sets are separated by ' *or* '.

From 19 December until the Epiphany and from the Monday of Holy Week until the Saturday of Easter Week, only seasonal psalms are provided.

Where more than one psalm is given, one psalm (printed in **bold**) may be used as the sole psalm at that office.

Guidance on how these options for saying the psalms are expressed typographically can be found in the 'Notes on the Lectionary' below.

A further cycle is provided (see table on page 85), which is largely the monthly sequential cycle of psalms given in the *Book of Common Prayer*.

A single psalm for use by those who only say one office each day is provided in Prayer During the Day in *Common Worship: Daily Prayer*.

An **Additional Weekday Lectionary**, intended particularly for use in places of worship that attract occasional rather than daily worshippers, is provided on pages 67–74. It can be used either at Morning or Evening Prayer. Psalmody is not provided and should be taken from provision outlined above.

Using the Lectionary tables

All **Bible references** (except to the Psalms) are to the *New Revised Standard Version* (New York, 1989). Those who use other Bible translations should check the verse numbers against the *NRSV*. Each reference gives book, chapter and verse, in that order.

References to the Psalms are to the Common Worship psalter, published in *Common Worship: Services and Prayers for the Church of England* (2000) and *Common Worship: Daily Prayer* (2005). A table showing the verse number differences between this and the psalter in the *Book of Common Prayer* is provided on the Common Worship website (https://www.churchofengland.org/prayer-worship/worship/texts/the-psalter/psalterverses.aspx).

Options in the provision of readings or psalms are presented in the following ways:
¶ square brackets [xx] give either optional additional verses or Psalms, or a shorter alternative;
¶ ' or ' indicates a simple choice between two alternative readings or courses of psalms;
¶ a psalm printed in **bold** may be used as the sole psalm at that office;
¶ on weekdays a psalm printed in parentheses (xx) is omitted if it has been used as the opening canticle at that office;
¶ a psalm marked with an asterisk may be shortened if desired.

Where a reading from the **Apocrypha** is offered, an alternative Old Testament reading is provided.

In the choice of **readings other than the Gospel** reading, the minister should ensure that, in any year, a balance is maintained between readings from the Old and New Testaments and that, where a particular biblical book is appointed to be read over several weeks, the choice ensures that the continuity of one book is not lost.

On the Sundays after Trinity, the Principal Service Lectionary provides **alternative Old Testament readings and psalms**. References in the left-hand column (under the heading 'Continuous') offer a *semi-continuous* reading of Old Testament texts. Such a reading and its complementary psalmody stand independently of the other readings. References in the right-hand column (under the heading 'Related') *relate* the Old Testament reading and the psalm to the Gospel reading. One column should be followed for the whole sequence of Sundays after Trinity.

The Lectionary 2018–2019

The Sunday and festal readings for 2 December 2018 (the First Sunday of Advent) to 30 November 2019 (the eve of Advent Sunday) are from **Year C**, which offers a semi-continuous reading of Luke's Gospel at the Principal Service on Sundays throughout the year.

The weekday readings for Holy Communion are from **Year One** of the Daily Eucharistic Lectionary (DEL).

Office readings are from Table 2 of the Weekday Lectionary at Morning Prayer: Old Testament 2a and New Testament 2 and from Table 1 of the Weekday Lectionary at Evening Prayer: Old Testament 1 and New Testament 1.

Notes on the Calendar 2 December 2018 — 30 November 2019

These notes are based on the Rules to Order the Christian Year (*Common Worship: Times and Seasons*, pages 24–30).

Sundays

All Sundays celebrate the paschal mystery of the death and resurrection of the Lord. They also reflect the character of the seasons in which they are set.

Principal Feasts

On these days (printed in **bold**) Holy Communion is celebrated in every cathedral and parish church, and this celebration, required by Canon B 14, may not be displaced by any other celebration, and may be dispensed with only in accordance with the provision of Canon B 14A.

Except in the case of Christmas Day and Easter Day, the celebration of the Feast *begins with Evening Prayer on the day before the Feast*, and the Collect at that Evening Prayer is that of the Feast. In the case of Christmas Eve and Easter Eve, there is proper liturgical provision (including a Collect) for the whole day.

The Presentation of Christ in the Temple (Candlemas) is celebrated on either Saturday 2 February or Sunday 3 February. **All Saints' Day** may be celebrated on Sunday 3 November (replacing the Fourth Sunday before Advent), with or without a supplementary celebration on Friday 1 November.

Other Principal Holy Days

These days (printed in **bold**), and the liturgical provision for them, may not be displaced by any other celebration.

Ash Wednesday (6 March) and **Maundy Thursday** (18 April) are Principal Holy Days. On both these days Holy Communion is celebrated in every cathedral or parish church, except where there is dispensation under Canon B 14A.

Good Friday (19 April) is a Principal Holy Day.

Eastertide

The paschal character of **the Great Fifty Days of Easter**, from Easter Day (21 April) to Pentecost (9 June), should be celebrated throughout the season, and should not be displaced by other celebrations. No Festival day may be celebrated in Easter Week; and nor may any Festival – except for a Patronal or Dedication Festival – displace the celebration of a Sunday (a memorial of the resurrection) during Eastertide. The paschal character of the season should be retained on those weekdays when saints' days are celebrated.

The three days before Ascension Day (27–29 May) are customarily observed as **Rogation Days**, when prayer is offered for God's blessing on the fruits of the earth and on human labour.

The nine days **after Ascension Day until the eve of Pentecost** (31 May–8 June) are observed as days of prayer and preparation for the celebration of the outpouring of the Holy Spirit.

Ordinary Time

Ordinary Time comprises two periods in the year: first, the period from the day after the Presentation of Christ in the Temple until the day before Ash Wednesday, and second, that from the day after Pentecost until the day before the First Sunday of Advent.

During Ordinary Time, there is no seasonal emphasis, except that the period between All Saints' Day and the First Sunday of Advent is a time to celebrate and reflect upon the reign of Christ in earth and heaven.

Festivals

These days (printed in roman), and the liturgical provision for them, are not usually displaced. For each day there is full liturgical provision for a Principal, Second and Third Service, and an optional so-called First Evening Prayer on the evening before the Festival where this is required.

Festivals may *not* be celebrated on Sundays in Advent, Lent or Eastertide, the Baptism of Christ, Ascension Day, Trinity Sunday or Christ the King, or weekdays between Palm Sunday and the Second Sunday of Easter.

Otherwise, a Festival falling on a Sunday – namely in 2018–19, Michael and All Angels (falling on the Fifteenth Sunday after Trinity) – may be kept on that Sunday or transferred to the Monday (or, at the discretion of the minister, to the next suitable weekday).

Certain Festivals (namely, Thomas the Apostle, Matthias the Apostle, the Visit of the Blessed Virgin Mary to Elizabeth, and the Blessed Virgin Mary) have customary alternative dates (see p.8).

The Thursday after Trinity Sunday (20 June) may be observed as the **Day of Thanksgiving for the Institution of Holy Communion** (sometimes known as *Corpus Christi*), and may be kept as a Festival.

Other Celebrations

Mothering Sunday falls on the Fourth Sunday of Lent (31 March). Alternative prayers and readings are provided for the Principal Service. **Bible Sunday** may be celebrated on 27 October, replacing the Last Sunday after Trinity, and appropriate prayers and readings are provided.

Local Celebrations

The celebration of **the patron saint or the title of a church** is kept either as a Festival or as a Principal Feast.

The **Dedication Festival** of a church is the anniversary of the date of its dedication or consecration. This is kept either as a Festival or as a Principal Feast. When kept as Principal Feasts, the Patronal and Dedication Festivals may be transferred to the nearest Sunday, unless that day is already a Principal Feast or one of the following days: the First Sunday of Advent, the Baptism of Christ, the First Sunday of Lent, the Fifth Sunday of Lent, or Palm Sunday. If the actual date is not known, the Dedication Festival may be celebrated on 6 October (replacing the Sixteenth Sunday after Trinity), or on 27 October (replacing the Last Sunday after Trinity), or on a suitable date chosen locally. Readings can be found on page 75.

Harvest Thanksgiving may be celebrated on any Sunday in autumn, replacing the provision for that day, provided it does not displace any Principal Feast or Festival.

Diocesan and other local provision may be made in **the calendar of the saints** to supplement the general calendar, in accordance with Canon B 6, paragraph 5.

Lesser Festivals

Lesser Festivals (printed in ordinary roman type, in black) are observed in a manner appropriate to a particular place. Each is provided with a Collect, which may supersede the Collect of the week. For certain Lesser Festivals a complete set of Eucharistic readings is provided, and for others appropriate readings may be selected from the Common of the Saints (see pages 77–81). These readings may, at the minister's discretion, supersede the Daily Eucharistic Lectionary (DEL). The weekday psalms and readings at Morning and Evening Prayer are not usually superseded by those for Lesser Festivals, but at the minister's discretion psalms and readings provided on these days for use at Holy Communion may be used instead at Morning or Evening Prayer.

The minister may be selective in the Lesser Festivals that are observed and may also keep some, or all of them, as Commemorations, perhaps especially in Advent, Lent and Easter where the character of the season ought to be sustained. If the Day of Thanksgiving for the Institution of Holy Communion (20 June) is not kept as a Festival in 2019, it may be kept as a Lesser Festival.

When a Lesser Festival falls on a Principal Feast or Holy Day, a Festival, a Sunday, or on a weekday between Palm Sunday and the Second Sunday of Easter, its celebration is normally omitted for that year. However, where there is sufficient reason, it may, at the discretion of the minister, be celebrated on the nearest available day.

Commemorations

Commemorations (printed in *italic*) are made by a mention in prayers of intercession. They are not provided with Collect, Psalm and Readings, and do not replace the usual weekday provision at Holy Communion or at Morning and Evening Prayer.

The minister may be selective in the Commemorations that are made.

Only where there is an established celebration in the wider Church or where the day has a special local significance may a Commemoration be observed as a Lesser Festival, with liturgical provision from the Common of the Saints (pages 77–81).

In designating a Commemoration as a Lesser Festival, the minister must remember the need to maintain the spirit of the season, especially of Advent, Lent and Easter.

Days of Discipline and Self-Denial

The weekdays of Lent and every Friday in the year are days of discipline and self-denial, with the exception of Principal Feasts, Festivals outside Lent, and Fridays from Easter Day to Pentecost. The day preceding a Principal Feast may also be appropriately kept as a day of discipline and self-denial in preparation for the Feast.

Ember Days

Ember Days should be kept, under the bishop's directions, in the week before an ordination as days of prayer for those to be ordained deacon or priest.

Ember Days may also be kept even when there is no ordination in the diocese as more general days of prayer for those who serve the Church in its various ministries, both ordained and lay, and for vocations. Traditionally they have been observed on the Wednesday, Friday and Saturday in the week before the Third Sunday of Advent, the Second Sunday of Lent, and the Sundays nearest to 29 June and 29 September.

Notes on Collects

For a table showing where the Collects and Post Communions are published, see page 75.

Where a Collect ends 'through Jesus Christ ... now and for ever', the minister may omit the longer (trinitarian) ending and use the shorter ending, 'through Jesus Christ our Lord', to which the people respond, 'Amen'. The longer ending, however, is to be preferred at a service of Holy Communion.

The Collect for each Sunday is used at Evening Prayer on the Saturday preceding, except where that Saturday is a Principal Feast, or a Festival, or the eve of Christmas Day or Easter Day. The Collect for each Sunday is also used on the weekdays following, except where other provision is made.

Abbreviations used in this book

Alt	Alternative
Bp	Bishop
BVM	Blessed Virgin Mary
DEL	Daily Eucharistic Lectionary
EP	Evening Prayer
G	Green
HC	Holy Communion: used where additional references are given to provide alternative texts for use at a celebration of Holy Communion (most often the provision of a psalm or gospel)
MP	Morning Prayer
P or p	Purple or Violet
P(La)	Purple or Lent Array
Ps & Pss	Psalmody
R or r	Red
W or w	White (Gold is indicated where its use would be appropriate)

Standard abbreviations have been used for other books of the Bible where necessary.

Alternative dates

The following may be celebrated on the alternative dates indicated:

Thomas the Apostle
– on 21 December 2018 instead of 3 July 2019

Matthias the Apostle
– on 24 February (or transferred to 25 February) instead of 14 May

The Visit of the Blessed Virgin Mary to Elizabeth
– on 2 July instead of 31 May

Cuthbert
– on 4 September instead of 20 March

The Blessed Virgin Mary
– on 8 September instead of 15 August

Chad
– with Cedd on 26 October instead of 2 March

If any of the four festivals is celebrated on the alternative date these provisions should be used on the principal date:

Holy Communion	Morning Prayer	Evening Prayer
If Thomas the Apostle is celebrated on Friday 21 December 2018 the following provision is used on Wednesday 3 July 2019 (G):		
Genesis 21.5, 8–20	Psalm 119.57–80	Psalms **59**, 60 (67)
Psalm 34.1–12	Ezra 4.1–5	Judges 5
Matthew 8.28–end	Romans 10.1–10	Luke 13.22–end
If Matthias the Apostle is celebrated on Sunday 24 February (or transferred to 25 February) the following provision is used on Tuesday 14 May (W):		
Acts 11.19–26	Psalm 139 or **48**, 52	Psalms 115, **116** or **50**
Psalm 87	Deuteronomy 9.23—10.5	Exodus 32.15–34
John 10.22–30	Ephesians 4.17–end	Luke 3.1–14
If The Visit of the Blessed Virgin Mary to Elizabeth is celebrated on Tuesday 2 July the following provision is used on Friday 31 May (W):		
Acts 18.9–18	Psalms 20, **81** or **88** (95)	Psalm **145** or **102**
Psalm 47.1–6	Deuteronomy 29.2–15	Numbers 20.1–13
John 16.20–23	1 John 1.1—2.6	Luke 7.11–17
If The Blessed Virgin Mary is celebrated on Sunday 8 September the following provision is used on Thursday 15 August (G):		
Joshua 3.7–11, 13–17	Psalm **37***	Psalms 39, **40**
Psalm 114	Jeremiah 33.14–end	1 Samuel 17.1–30
Matthew 18.21—19.1	James 4.1–12	Luke 23.56b—24.12

Key to the Tables

For guidance on how the options for saying the psalms are expressed typographically, see page 5.

Sundays (and Principal Feasts, other Principal Holy Days, and Festivals)

Day	Date		Principal Service	3rd Service	2nd Service
	Sunday / **Feast** † / Festival ††	*Colour*	Main service of the day: Holy Communion, Morning Prayer, Evening Prayer, or a Service of the Word	Shorter Readings, an Office lectionary probably used at Morning Prayer where Holy Communion is the Principal Service	2nd main Service, probably used at Evening Prayer; adaptable for Holy Communion

† Principal Feasts and other Principal Holy Days are printed in **bold**.
†† Festivals are printed in roman typeface.

Weekdays

Day	Date		Holy Communion	Morning Prayer	Evening Prayer
		Colour	Weekday readings	Psalms and readings for Morning Prayer	Psalms and readings for Evening Prayer

‡ Lesser Festival ‡* [optional]
‡‡ *Commemoration* ‡‡ [optional]

‡ Lesser Festivals are printed in roman typeface, in black.
‡‡ Commemorations are printed in *italics*.
* The ascriptions given to holy men and women in the Calendar (such as martyr; teacher of the faith, etc.) have often been abbreviated in this booklet for reasons of space. The particular ascription given is there to be helpful if needing to choose Collects and readings from Common of the Saints; where several ascriptions are used (e.g. bishop and martyr), traditionally the last ascription given is the most important and therefore the guiding one. The full ascriptions may be found in the Calendar, which is printed in *Common Worship: Times and Seasons* (pages 7–22), *Common Worship: Festivals* (pages 5–20) and *Common Worship: Daily Prayer* (pages 5–16). These incorporate minor corrections made since the publication of the Calendar in *Common Worship: Services and Prayers for the Church of England* (pages 5–16).

Advent 1

		Principal Service	3rd Service	2nd Service
Sunday	**2 December** **1st Sunday of Advent** ᴾ	Jeremiah 33.14–16 Psalm 25.1–9 1 Thessalonians 3.9–end Luke 21.25–36	Psalm 44 Isaiah 51.4–11 Romans 13.11–end	Psalm 9 [or 9.1–8] Joel 3.9–end Revelation 14.13—15.4 HC John 3.1–17
		Holy Communion	**Morning Prayer**	**Evening Prayer**
Monday	**3 December** ᴾ *Francis Xavier, missionary, 1552*	Isaiah 2.1–5 Psalm 122 Matthew 8.5–11	Psalms **50**, 54 or 1, 2, 3 Isaiah 42.18–end Revelation 19	Psalms 70, **71** or **4**, 7 Isaiah 25.1–9 Matthew 12.1–21
Tuesday	**4 December** ᴾ *John of Damascus, monk, teacher of the faith, c.749 Nicholas Ferrar, deacon, founder of the Little Gidding Community, 1637*	Isaiah 11.1–10 Psalm 72.1–4, 18–19 Luke 10.21–24	Psalms **80**, 82 or **5**, 6 (8) Isaiah 43.1–13 Revelation 20	Psalms **74**, 75 or **9**, 10* Isaiah 26.1–13 Matthew 12.22–37
Wednesday	**5 December** ᴾ	Isaiah 25.6–10a Psalm 23 Matthew 15.29–37	Psalms 5, **7** or 119.1–32 Isaiah 43.14–end Revelation 21.1–8	Psalms 76, **77** or **11**, 12, 13 Isaiah 28.1–13 Matthew 12.38–end
Thursday	**6 December** ᴾʷ *Nicholas, bishop, c.326 (see p.79)*	Isaiah 26.1–6 Psalm 118.18–27a Matthew 7.21, 24–27	Psalms **42**, 43 or 14, **15**, 16 Isaiah 44.1–8 Revelation 21.9–21	Psalms **40**, 46 or **18*** Isaiah 28.14–end Matthew 13.1–23
Friday	**7 December** ᴾʷ *Ambrose, bishop, teacher of the faith, 397 (see p.78)*	Isaiah 29.17–end Psalm 27.1–4, 16–17 Matthew 9.27–31	Psalms **25**, 26 or 17, **19** Isaiah 44.9–23 Revelation 21.22—22.5	Psalms 16, **17** or **22** Isaiah 29.1–14 Matthew 13.24–43
Saturday	**8 December** ᴾʷ *Conception of the Blessed Virgin Mary (see p.77)*	Isaiah 30.19–21, 23–26 Psalm 146.4–9 Matthew 9.35—10.1, 6–8	Psalms **9** (10) or 20, 21, **23** Isaiah 44.24—45.13 Revelation 22.6–end	Psalms **27**, 28 or **24**, 25 Isaiah 29.15–end Matthew 13.44–end

Advent 2

		Principal Service	3rd Service	2nd Service
Sunday	**9 December** P **2nd Sunday of Advent**	Baruch 5 or Malachi 3.1–4 *Canticle:* Benedictus Philippians 1.3–11 Luke 3.1–6	Psalm 80 Isaiah 64.1–7 Matthew 11.2–11	Psalms 75 [76] Isaiah 40.1–11 Luke 1.1–25
		Holy Communion	**Morning Prayer**	**Evening Prayer**
Monday	**10 December** P	Isaiah 35 Psalm 85.7–end Luke 5.17–26	Psalm **44** or 27, **30** Isaiah 45.14–end 1 Thessalonians 1	Psalms **144**, 146 or 26, **28, 29** Isaiah 30.1–18 Matthew 14.1–12
Tuesday	**11 December** P	Isaiah 40.1–11 Psalm 96.1, 10–end Matthew 18.12–14	Psalms **56**, 57 or 32, **36** Isaiah 46 1 Thessalonians 2.1–12	Psalms **11**, 12, 13 or **33** Isaiah 30.19–end Matthew 14.13–end
Wednesday	**12 December** P Ember Day	Isaiah 40.25–end Psalm 103.8–13 Matthew 11.28–end	Psalms **62**, 63 or **34** Isaiah 47 1 Thessalonians 2.13–end	Psalms 10, 14 or 1**19.33–56** Isaiah 31 Matthew 15.1–20
Thursday	**13 December** Pr Lucy, martyr, 304 (see p.77) *Samuel Johnson, moralist, 1784*	Isaiah 41.13–20 Psalm 145.1, 8–13 Matthew 11.11–15	Psalms 53, **54**, 60 or **37*** Isaiah 48.1–11 1 Thessalonians 3	Psalm **73** or 39, **40** Isaiah 32 Matthew 15.21–28
Friday	**14 December** Pw John of the Cross, poet, teacher of the faith, 1591 (see p.78) Ember Day	Isaiah 48.17–19 Psalm 1 Matthew 11.16–19	Psalms 85, **86** or **31** Isaiah 48.12–end 1 Thessalonians 4.1–12	Psalms 82, **90** or **35** Isaiah 33.1–22 Matthew 15.29–end
Saturday	**15 December** P Ember Day	Ecclesiasticus 48.1–4, 9–11 or 2 Kings 2.9–12 Psalm 80.1–4, 18–19 Matthew 17.10–13	Psalm **145** or 41, **42**, 43 Isaiah 49.1–13 1 Thessalonians 4.13–end	Psalms 93, **94** or 45, **46** Isaiah 35 Matthew 16.1–12

Advent 3

		Principal Service	3rd Service	2nd Service
Sunday	**16 December** P **3rd Sunday of Advent**	Zephaniah 3.14–end *Canticle:* Isaiah 12.2–end [*or* Psalm 146.4–end] Philippians 4.4–7 Luke 3.7–18	Psalms 12, 14 Isaiah 25.1–9 1 Corinthians 4.1–5	Psalms 50.1–6 [62] Isaiah 35 Luke 1.57–66 [67–end]
		Holy Communion	**Morning Prayer**	**Evening Prayer**
Monday	**17 December** P *O Sapientia* *Eglantyne Jebb, social reformer,* *founder of 'Save The Children', 1928*	Genesis 49.2, 8–10 Psalm 72.1–5 Matthew 1.1–17	Psalm **40** *or* **44** Isaiah 49.14–25 1 Thessalonians 5.1–11	Psalms 25, **26** *or* **47**, 49 Isaiah 38.1–8, 21–22 Matthew 16.13–end
Tuesday	**18 December** P	Jeremiah 23.5–8 Psalm 72.1–2, 12–13, 18–end Matthew 1.18–24	Psalms **70**, 74 *or* **48**, 52 Isaiah 50 1 Thessalonians 5.12–end	Psalms **50**, 54 *or* **50** Isaiah 38.9–20 Matthew 17.1–13
			From Wednesday 19 December until the Epiphany *the seasonal psalmody must be used at Morning and Evening Prayer*	
Wednesday	**19 December** P	Judges 13.2–7, 24–end Psalm 71.3–8 Luke 1.5–25	Psalms 144, **146** Isaiah 51.1–8 2 Thessalonians 1	Psalms 10, **57** Isaiah 39 Matthew 17.14–21
Thursday	**20 December** P	Isaiah 7.10–14 Psalm 24.1–6 Luke 1.26–38	Psalms **46**, 95 Isaiah 51.9–16 2 Thessalonians 2	Psalms **4**, 9 Zephaniah 1.1—2.3 Matthew 17.22–end
Friday	**21 December** P	Zephaniah 3.14–18 Psalm 33.1–4, 11–12, 20–end Luke 1.39–45	Psalms **121**, 122, 123 Isaiah 51.17–end 2 Thessalonians 3	Psalms 80, **84** Zephaniah 3.1–13 Matthew 18.1–20
Saturday	**22 December** P	1 Samuel 1.24–end Psalm 113 Luke 1.46–56	Psalms **124**, 125, 126, 127 Isaiah 52.1–12 Jude	Psalms 24, **48** Zephaniah 3.14–end Matthew 18.21–end

Advent 4 / Christmas

		Principal Service	3rd Service	2nd Service
Sunday	**23 December** **4th Sunday of Advent** P	Micah 5.2–5a Canticle: Magnificat or Psalm 80.1–8 Hebrews 10.5–10 Luke 1.39–45 [46–55]	Psalm 144 Isaiah 32.1–8 Revelation 22.6–end	Psalms 123 [131] Isaiah 10.33—11.10 Matthew 1.18–end
		Holy Communion	**Morning Prayer**	**Evening Prayer**
Monday	**24 December** **Christmas Eve** P	Morning Eucharist only: 2 Samuel 7.1–5, 8–11, 16 Psalm 89.2, 19–27 Acts 13.16–26 Luke 1.67–79	Psalms **45**, 113 Isaiah 52.13—end of 53 2 Peter 1.1–15	Psalm **85** Zechariah 2 Revelation 1.1–8
		Principal Service	**3rd Service**	**2nd Service**
Tuesday	**25 December** **Christmas Day** Gold or W	Any of the following three sets of Principal Service readings may be used on the evening of Christmas Eve and on Christmas Day. Set III should be used at some service during the celebration. **Set I** Isaiah 9.2–7 Psalm 96 Titus 2.11–14 Luke 2.1–14 [15–20] **Set II** Isaiah 62.6–end Psalm 97 Titus 3.4–7 Luke 2. [1–7] 8–20 **Set III** Isaiah 52.7–10 Psalm 98 Hebrews 1.1–4 [5–12] John 1.1–14	MP Psalms **110**, 117 Isaiah 62.1–5 Matthew 1.18–end	EP Psalm 8 Isaiah 65.17–25 Philippians 2.5–11 or Luke 2.1–20 if it has not been used at the principal service of the day
Wednesday	**26 December** Stephen, deacon, first martyr R	2 Chronicles 24.20–22 or Acts 7.51–end Psalm 119.161–168 Acts 7.51–end or Galatians 2.16b–20 Matthew 10.17–22	EP Psalms 57, **86** Genesis 4.1–10 Matthew 23.34–end	
Thursday	**27 December** John, Apostle and Evangelist W	Exodus 33.7–11a Psalm 117 1 John 1 John 21.19b–end	MP Psalms **13**, 31.1–8, 150 Jeremiah 26.12–15 Acts 6	
Friday	**28 December** The Holy Innocents R	Jeremiah 31.15–17 Psalm 124 1 Corinthians 1.26–29 Matthew 2.13–18	MP Psalms 21, 147.13–end Exodus 33.12–end 1 John 2.1–11	EP Psalm 97 Isaiah 6.1–8 1 John 5.1–12
		Holy Communion	**Morning Prayer**	**Evening Prayer**
Saturday	**29 December** Thomas Becket, archbishop, martyr, 1170 (see p.77) Wr	1 John 2.3–11 Psalm 96.1–4 Luke 2.22–35	MP Psalms **36**, 146 Baruch 4.21–27 or Genesis 37.13–20 Matthew 18.1–10 Psalms **19**, 20 Isaiah 57.15–end John 1.1–18	EP Psalms 123, **128** Isaiah 49.14–25 Mark 10.13–16 Psalms 131, **132** Jonah 1 Colossians 1.1–14

Christmas 1

		Principal Service	3rd Service	2nd Service
Sunday	**30 December** W 1st Sunday of Christmas	1 Samuel 2.18–20, 26 Psalm 148 [or 148.7–end] Colossians 3.12–17 Luke 2.41–end	Psalm 105.1–11 Isaiah 41.21—42.1 1 John 1.1–7	Psalm 132 Isaiah 61 Galatians 3.27—4.7 HC Luke 2.15–21
		Holy Communion	**Morning Prayer**	**Evening Prayer**
Monday	**31 December** W *John Wyclif, reformer, 1384*	1 John 2.18–21 Psalm 96.1, 11–end John 1.1–18	Psalm 102 Isaiah 59.15b–end John 1.29–34	Psalms 90, 148 Jonah 3–4 Colossians 1.24—2.7 *or:* 1st EP of the Naming and Circumcision of Jesus: Psalm 148; Jeremiah 23.1–6; Colossians 2.8–15
		Principal Service	**3rd Service**	**2nd Service**
Tuesday	**1 January** W Naming and Circumcision of Jesus	Numbers 6.22–end Psalm 8 Galatians 4.4–7 Luke 2.15–21	MP Psalms **103**, 150 Genesis 17.1–13 Romans 2.17–end	EP Psalm **115** Deuteronomy 30.[1–10] 11–end Acts 3.1–16
		Holy Communion	**Morning Prayer**	**Evening Prayer**
Wednesday	**2 January** W Basil the Great and Gregory of Nazianzus, bishops, teachers of the faith, 379 and 389 (see p.78) *Seraphim, monk, spiritual guide, 1833* *Vedanayagam Samuel Azariah,* *bishop, evangelist, 1945*	1 John 2.22–28 Psalm 98.1–4 John 1.19–28	Psalm **18**.1–30 Isaiah 60.1–12 John 1.35–42	Psalms 45, **46** Ruth 1 Colossians 2.8–end
Thursday	**3 January** W	1 John 2.29—3.6 Psalm 98.2–7 John 1.29–34	Psalms **127**, 128, 131 Isaiah 60.13–end John 1.43–end	Psalms **2**, 110 Ruth 2 Colossians 3.1–11
Friday	**4 January** W	1 John 3. 7–10 Psalm 98.1, 8–end John 1.35–42	Psalm **89**.1–37 Isaiah 61 John 2.1–12	Psalms 85, **87** Ruth 3 Colossians 3.12—4.1
Saturday	**5 January** W	1 John 3.11–21 Psalm 100 John 1.43–end	Psalms 8, **48** Isaiah 62 John 2.13–end	**1st EP of the Epiphany:** Psalms 96, **97** Isaiah 49.1–13 John 4.7–26

Epiphany

		Principal Service	3rd Service	2nd Service
Sunday	**6 January** **Epiphany** *Gold or W*	Isaiah 60.1–6 Psalm 72. [1–9] 10–15 Ephesians 3.1–12 Matthew 2.1–12	MP Psalms **132**, 113 Jeremiah 31.7–14 John 1.29–34	EP Psalms **98**, 100 Baruch 4.36—end of 5 or Isaiah 60.1–9 John 2.1–11
		Holy Communion	**Morning Prayer**	**Evening Prayer**
Monday	**7 January** *W*	1 John 3.22—4.6 Psalm 72.7–end Matthew 4.12–17, 23–end	Psalms **99**, 147.1–12 or **71** Isaiah 63.7–end 1 John 3	Psalm **118** or **72**, 75 Baruch 1.15—2.10 or Jeremiah 23.1–8 Matthew 20.1–16
Tuesday	**8 January** *W*	1 John 4.7–10 Psalm 72.1–8 Mark 6.34–44	Psalms **46**, 147.13–end or **73** Isaiah 64 1 John 4.7–end	Psalm **145** or **74** Baruch 2.11–end or Jeremiah 30.1–17 Matthew 20.17–28
Wednesday	**9 January** *W*	1 John 4.11–18 Psalm 72.1, 10–13 Mark 6.45–52	Psalms 2, **148** or **77** Isaiah 65.1–16 1 John 5.1–12	Psalms **67**, 72 or **119.81–104** Baruch 3.1–8 or Jeremiah 30.18—31.9 Matthew 20.29–end
Thursday	**10 January** *W* *William Laud, archbishop, 1645*	1 John 4.19—5.4 Psalm 72.1, 17–end Luke 4.14–22	Psalms 97, **149** or **78.1–39*** Isaiah 65.17–end 1 John 5.13–end	Psalms 27, **29** or **78.40–end*** Baruch 3.9—4.4 or Jeremiah 31.10–17 Matthew 23.1–12
Friday	**11 January** *W* *Mary Slessor, missionary, 1915*	1 John 5.5–13 Psalm 147.13–end Luke 5.12–16	Psalms 98, **150** or **55** Isaiah 66.1–11 2 John	Psalms **93**, 132 or **69** Baruch 4.21–30 or Jeremiah 33.14–end Matthew 23.13–28
Saturday	**12 January** *W* Aelred, abbot, 1167 (see p.80) Benedict Biscop, scholar, 689	1 John 5.14–end Psalm 149.1–5 John 3.22–30	Psalms **96**, 145 or **76**, 79 Isaiah 66.12–23 3 John	**1st EP of the Baptism of Christ** Psalm 36 Isaiah 61 Titus 2.11–14; 3.4–7

Baptism of Christ (Epiphany 2)

		Principal Service	3rd Service	2nd Service
Sunday	**13 January** W Baptism of Christ 2nd Sunday of Epiphany	Isaiah 43.1–7 Psalm 29 Acts 8.14–17 Luke 3.15–17, 21–22	Psalm 89.19–29 Isaiah 42.1–9 Acts 19.1–7	Psalms 46, 47 Isaiah 55.1–11 Romans 6.1–11 HC Mark 1.4–11
		Holy Communion	**Morning Prayer**	**Evening Prayer**
Monday	**14 January** W DEL week 1	Hebrews 1.1–6 Psalm 97.1–2, 6–10 Mark 1.14–20	Psalms 2, 110 or 80, 82 Amos 1 1 Corinthians 1.1–17	Psalms 34, 36 or 85, 86 Genesis 1.1–19 Matthew 21.1–17
Tuesday	**15 January** W	Hebrews 2.5–12 Psalm 8 Mark 1.21–28	Psalms 8, 9 or 87, 89.1–18 Amos 2 1 Corinthians 1.18–end	Psalms 45, 46 or 89.19–end Genesis 1.20—2.3 Matthew 21.18–32
Wednesday	**16 January** W	Hebrews 2.14–end Psalm 105.1–9 Mark 1.29–39	Psalms 19, 20 or 119.105–128 Amos 3 1 Corinthians 2	Psalms 47, 48 or 91, 93 Genesis 2.4–end Matthew 21.33–end
Thursday	**17 January** W Antony of Egypt, hermit, abbot, 356 (see p.80) Charles Gore, bishop, founder of the Community of the Resurrection, 1932	Hebrews 3.7–14 Psalm 95.1, 8–end Mark 1.40–end	Psalms 21, 24 or 90, 92 Amos 4 1 Corinthians 3	Psalms 61, 65 or 94 Genesis 3 Matthew 22.1–14
Friday	**18 January** W Week of Prayer for Christian Unity: 18–25 January Amy Carmichael, founder of the Dohnavour foundation, spiritual writer, 1951	Hebrews 4.1–5, 11 Psalm 78.3–8 Mark 2.1–12	Psalms 67, 72 or 88 (95) Amos 5.1–17 1 Corinthians 4	Psalm 68 or 102 Genesis 4.1–16, 25–26 Matthew 22.15–33
Saturday	**19 January** W Wulfstan, bishop, 1095 (see p.79)	Hebrews 4.12–end Psalm 19.7–end Mark 2.13–17	Psalms 29, 33 or 96, 97, 100 Amos 5.18–end 1 Corinthians 5	Psalms 84, 85 or 104 Genesis 6.1–10 Matthew 22.34–end

Epiphany 3

		Principal Service	3rd Service	2nd Service
Sunday	**20 January** W 3rd Sunday of Epiphany	Isaiah 62.1–5 Psalm 36.5–10 1 Corinthians 12.1–11 John 2.1–11	Psalm 145.1–13 Isaiah 49.1–7 Acts 16.11–15	Psalm 96 1 Samuel 3.1–20 Ephesians 4.1–16 HC John 1.29–42
		Holy Communion	**Morning Prayer**	**Evening Prayer**
Monday	**21 January** Wr Agnes, child martyr, 304 (see p.77) DEL week 2	Hebrews 5.1–10 Psalm 110.1–4 Mark 2.18–22	Psalms 145, **146** or **98**, 99, 101 Amos 6 1 Corinthians 6.1–11	Psalm **71** or **105*** (or 103) Genesis 6.11—7.10 Matthew 24.1–14
Tuesday	**22 January** W *Vincent of Saragossa, deacon, martyr, 304*	Hebrews 6.10–end Psalm 111 Mark 2.23–end	Psalms **132**, 147.1–12 or **106*** (or 103) Amos 7 1 Corinthians 6.12–end	Psalm **89**.1–37 or**107*** Genesis 7.11–end Matthew 24.15–28
Wednesday	**23 January** W	Hebrews 7.1–3, 15–17 Psalm 110.1–4 Mark 3.1–6	Psalms 81, 147.13–end or 110, **111**, 112 Amos 8 1 Corinthians 7.1–24	Psalms **97**, 98 or 119.**129–152** Genesis 8.1–14 Matthew 24.29–end
Thursday	**24 January** W Francis de Sales, bishop, teacher of the faith, 1622 (see p.78)	Hebrews 7.25—8.6 Psalm 40.7–10, 17–end Mark 3.7–12	Psalms **76**, 148 or 113, **115** Amos 9 1 Corinthians 7.25–end	Psalms 99, 100, **111** or 114, **116**, 117 Genesis 8.15—9.7 Matthew 25.1–13 *or:* 1st EP of the Conversion of Paul: Psalm 149; Isaiah 49.1–13; Acts 22.3–16
		Principal Service	**3rd Service**	**2nd Service**
Friday	**25 January** W Conversion of Paul	Jeremiah 1.4–10 or Acts 9.1–22 Psalm 67 Acts 9.1–22 or Galatians 1.11–16a Matthew 19.27–end	MP Psalms 66, 147.13–end Ezekiel 3.22–end Philippians 3.1–14	EP Psalm 119.41–56 Ecclesiasticus 39.1–10 or Isaiah 56.1–8 Colossians 1.24—2.7
		Holy Communion	**Morning Prayer**	**Evening Prayer**
Saturday	**26 January** W Timothy and Titus, companions of Paul	Hebrews 9.2–3, 11–14 Psalm 47.1–8 Mark 3.20–21 *Lesser Festival eucharistic lectionary:* Isaiah 61.1–3a Psalm 100 2 Timothy 2.1–8 or Titus 1.1–5 Luke 10.1–9	Psalms **122**, 128, 150 or 120, **121**, 122 Hosea 2.2–17 1 Corinthians 9.1–14	Psalms **61**, 66 or **118** Genesis 11.1–9 Matthew 25.31–end

17

Epiphany 4 / Presentation

		Principal Service	3rd Service	2nd Service
Sunday	**27 January** W **4th Sunday of Epiphany**	Nehemiah 8.1–3, 5–6, 8–10 Psalm 19 [or 19.1–6] 1 Corinthians 12.12–31a Luke 4.14–21	Psalm 113 Deuteronomy 30.11–15 3 John 1, 5–8	Psalm 33 [or 33.1–12] Numbers 9.15–end 1 Corinthians 7.17–24 HC Mark 1.21–28
		Holy Communion	**Morning Prayer**	**Evening Prayer**
Monday	**28 January** W Thomas Aquinas, priest, philosopher, teacher of the faith, 1274 (see p.78) DEL week 3	Hebrews 9.15, 24–end Psalm 98.1–7 Mark 3. 22–30	Psalms 40, 108 or 123, 124, 125, 126 Hosea 2.18–end of 3 1 Corinthians 9.15–end	Psalms 138, 144 or 127, 128, 129 Genesis 11.27—12.9 Matthew 26.1–16
Tuesday	**29 January** W	Hebrews 10.1–10 Psalm 40.1–4, 7–10 Mark 3.31–end	Psalms 34, 36 or 132, 133 Hosea 4.1–16 1 Corinthians 10.1–13	Psalm 145 or (134,) 135 Genesis 13.2–end Matthew 26.17–35
Wednesday	**30 January** Wr Charles, king and martyr, 1649 (see p.77)	Hebrews 10.11–18 Psalm 110.1–4 Mark 4.1–20	Psalms 45, 46 or 119.153–end Hosea 5.1–7 1 Corinthians 10.14—11.1	Psalms 21, 29 or 136 Genesis 14 Matthew 26.36–46
Thursday	**31 January** W John Bosco, priest, founder of the Salesian Teaching Order, 1888	Hebrews 10.19–25 Psalm 24.1–6 Mark 4. 21–25	Psalms 47, 48 or 143, 146 Hosea 5.8—6.6 1 Corinthians 11.2–16	Psalms 24, 33 or 138, 140, 141 Genesis 15 Matthew 26.47–56
Friday	**1 February** W Brigid, abbess, c.525	Hebrews 10.32–end Psalm 37.3–6, 40–end Mark 4.26–34	Psalms 61, 65 or 142, 144 Hosea 6.7—7.2 1 Corinthians 11.17–end	Psalms 62, 77 or 145 Genesis 16 Matthew 26.57–end

or, if the Presentation of Christ is celebrated on Saturday 2 February:
1st EP of the Presentation:
Psalm 118; 1 Samuel 1.19b–end;
Hebrews 4.11–end

		Principal Service	3rd Service	2nd Service
Saturday	**2 February** *Gold or W* **Presentation of Christ in the Temple** (Candlemas)	Malachi 3.1–5 Psalm 24. [1–6] 7–end Hebrews 2.14–end Luke 2.22–40	MP Psalms 48, 146 Exodus 13.1–16 Romans 12.1–5	EP Psalms 122, 132 Haggai 2.1–9 John 2.18–22

or, if the Presentation of Christ is celebrated on Sunday 3 February:

		Holy Communion	Morning Prayer	Evening Prayer
Saturday	**2 February** W	Hebrews 11.1–2, 8–19 Canticle: Luke 1.69–73 Mark 4.35–end	Psalm 68 or 147 Hosea 14 1 Corinthians 12.1–11	1st EP of the Presentation: Psalm 118 1 Samuel 1.19b–end Hebrews 4.11–end

5 before Lent / Presentation

		Principal Service	3rd Service	2nd Service
Sunday	**3 February** G **5th Sunday before Lent** Ordinary Time begins today if the Presentation was celebrated on 2 February.	Ezekiel 43.27—44.4 Psalm 48 1 Corinthians 13 Luke 2.22–40	Psalm 71.1–6, 15–17 Micah 6.1–8 1 Corinthians 6.12–20	Psalm 34 1 Chronicles 29.6–19 Acts 7.44–50 *HC* John 4.19–29*a*
or **Sunday**	**3 February** Gold or W **Presentation of Christ in the Temple** (Candlemas)	Malachi 3.1–5 Psalm 24. [1–6] 7–end Hebrews 2.14–end Luke 2.22–40	*MP* Psalms **48**, 146 Exodus 13.1–16 Romans 12.1–5	*EP* Psalms 122, **132** Haggai 2.1–9 John 2.18–22
		Holy Communion	**Morning Prayer**	**Evening Prayer**
Monday	**4 February** G *Gilbert, founder of the Gilbertine Order, 1189* DEL week 4	Hebrews 11.32–end Psalm 31.19–end Mark 5.1–20	Psalms 1, **2**, 3 1 Chronicles 10.1—11.9 John 13.1–11	Psalms **4**, 7 Exodus 22.21–27, 23.1–17 Philippians 1.1–11
Tuesday	**5 February** G	Hebrews 12.1–4 Psalm 22.25*b*–end Mark 5.21–43	Psalms **5**, 6 (8) 1 Chronicles 13 John 13.12–20	Psalms **9**, 10* Exodus 29.38—30.16 Philippians 1.12–end
Wednesday	**6 February** G *Martyrs of Japan, 1597* *Accession of Queen Elizabeth II, 1952 (see p.83)*	Hebrews 12.4–7, 11–15 Psalm 103.1–2, 13–18 Mark 6.1–6*a*	Psalm 1**19.1–32** 1 Chronicles 15.1—16.3 John 13.21–30	Psalms **11**, 12, 13 Leviticus 8 Philippians 2.1–13
Thursday	**7 February** G	Hebrews 12.18–19, 21–24 Psalm 48.1–3, 8–10 Mark 6.7–13	Psalms 14, **15**, 16 1 Chronicles 17 John 13.31–end	Psalm **18*** Leviticus 9 Philippians 2.14–end
Friday	**8 February** G	Hebrews 13.1–8 Psalm 27.1–6, 9–12 Mark 6.14–29	Psalms 17, **19** 1 Chronicles 21.1–22.1 John 14.1–14	Psalm **22** Leviticus 16.2–24 Philippians 3.1—4.1
Saturday	**9 February** G	Hebrews 13.15–17, 20–21 Psalm 23 Mark 6.30–34	Psalms 20, 21, **23** 1 Chronicles 22.2–end John 14.15–end	Psalms **24**, 25 Leviticus 17 Philippians 4.2–end

4 before Lent

		Principal Service	3rd Service	2nd Service
Sunday	**10 February** G **4th Sunday before Lent** Proper 1	Isaiah 6.1–8 [9–end] Psalm 138 1 Corinthians 15.1–11 Luke 5.1–11	Psalms 3, 4 Jeremiah 26.1–16 Acts 3.1–10	Psalms [1] 2 Wisdom 6.1–21 or Hosea 1 Colossians 3.1–22 HC Matthew 5.13–20
		Holy Communion	**Morning Prayer**	**Evening Prayer**
Monday	**11 February** G DEL week 5	Genesis 1.1–19 Psalm 104.1–2, 6–13, 26 Mark 6.53–end	Psalms 27, **30** 1 Chronicles 28.1–10 John 15.1–11	Psalms 26, **28**, 29 Leviticus 19.1–18, 30–end 1 Timothy 1.1–17
Tuesday	**12 February** G	Genesis 1.20—2.4a Psalm 8 Mark 7.1–13	Psalms 32, **36** 1 Chronicles 28.11–end John 15.12–17	Psalm **33** Leviticus 23.1–22 1 Timothy 1.18—end of 2
Wednesday	**13 February** G	Genesis 2.4b–9, 15–17 Psalm 104.11–12, 29–32 Mark 7.14–23	Psalm **34** 1 Chronicles 29.1–9 John 15.18–end	Psalm 1**19.33–56** Leviticus 23.23–end 1 Timothy 3
Thursday	**14 February** Gw Cyril and Methodius, missionaries, 869 and 885 (see p.80) *Valentine, martyr at Rome, c.269*	Genesis 2.18–end Psalm 128 Mark 7.24–30	Psalm **37*** 1 Chronicles 29.10–20 John 16.1–15	Psalms 39, **40** Leviticus 24.1–9 1 Timothy 4
Friday	**15 February** G *Sigfrid, bishop, 1045* *Thomas Bray, priest,* *founder of SPCK and SPG, 1730*	Genesis 3.1–8 Psalm 32.1–8 Mark 7.31–end	Psalm **31** 1 Chronicles 29.21–end John 16.16–22	Psalm **35** Leviticus 25.1–24 1 Timothy 5.1–16
Saturday	**16 February** G	Genesis 3.9–end Psalm 90.1–12 Mark 8.1–10	Psalms 41, **42**, 43 2 Chronicles 1.1–13 John 16.23–end	Psalms 45, **46** Numbers 6.1–5, 21–end 1 Timothy 5.17–end

3 before Lent

		Principal Service	3rd Service	2nd Service
Sunday	**17 February** G **3rd Sunday before Lent** Proper 2	Jeremiah 17.5–10 Psalm 1 1 Corinthians 15.12–20 Luke 6.17–26	Psalm 7 Jeremiah 30.1–3, 10–22 Acts 6	Psalms [5] 6 Wisdom 11.21—12.11 or Hosea 10.1–8, 12 Galatians 4.8–20 HC Matthew 5.21–37
		Holy Communion	**Morning Prayer**	**Evening Prayer**
Monday	**18 February** G DEL week 6	Genesis 4.1–15, 25 Psalm 50.1, 8, 16–end Mark 8.11–13	Psalm **44** 2 Chronicles 2.1–16 John 17.1–5	Psalms **47**, 49 Genesis 24.1–28 1 Timothy 6.1–10
Tuesday	**19 February** G	Genesis 6.5–8; 7.1–5, 10 Psalm 29 Mark 8.14–21	Psalms **48**, 52 2 Chronicles 3 John 17.6–19	Psalm **50** Genesis 24.29–end 1 Timothy 6.11–end
Wednesday	**20 February** G	Genesis 8.6–13, 20–end Psalm 116.10–end Mark 8.22–26	Psalm 119.**57–80** 2 Chronicles 5 John 17.20–end	Psalms **59**, 60 (67) Genesis 25.7–11, 19–end 2 Timothy 1.1–14
Thursday	**21 February** G	Genesis 9.1–13 Psalm 102.16–23 Mark 8.27–33	Psalms 56, **57** (63*) 2 Chronicles 6.1–21 John 18.1–11	Psalms 61, **62**, 64 Genesis 26.34—27.40 2 Timothy 1.15—2.13
Friday	**22 February** G	Genesis 11.1–9 Psalm 33.10–15 Mark 8.34—9.1	Psalms 51, **54** 2 Chronicles 6.22–end John 18.12–27	Psalm **38** Genesis 27.41—end of 28 2 Timothy 2.14–end
Saturday	**23 February** Gr Polycarp, bishop, martyr, c.155 (see p.77)	Hebrews 11.1–7 Psalm 145.1–10 Mark 9.2–13	Psalm **68** 2 Chronicles 7 John 18.28–end	Psalms 65, **66** Genesis 29.1–30 2 Timothy 3

2 before Lent

		Principal Service	3rd Service	2nd Service
Sunday	24 February G 2nd Sunday before Lent	Genesis 2.4b–9, 15–end Psalm 65 Revelation 4 Luke 8.22–25	Psalm 104.1–26 Job 28.1–11 Acts 14.8–17	Psalm 147 [or 147.13–end] Genesis 1.1—2.3 Matthew 6.25–end
		Holy Communion	Morning Prayer	Evening Prayer
Monday	25 February G DEL week 7	Ecclesiasticus 1.1–10 or James 1.1–11 Psalm 93 or 119.65–72 Mark 9.14–29	Psalm 71 2 Chronicles 9.1–12 John 19.1–16	Psalms 72, 75 Genesis 29.31—30.24 2 Timothy 4.1–8
Tuesday	26 February G	Ecclesiasticus 2.1–11 or James 1.12–18 Psalm 37.3–6, 27–28 or 94.12–18 Mark 9.30–37	Psalm 73 2 Chronicles 10.1—11.4 John 19.17–30	Psalm 74 Genesis 31.1–24 2 Timothy 4.9–end
Wednesday	27 February Gw George Herbert, priest, poet, 1633 (see p.79)	Ecclesiasticus 4.11–19 or James 1.19–end Psalm 119.161–168 or 15 Mark 9.38–40	Psalm 77 2 Chronicles 12 John 19.31–end	Psalm 119.81–104 Genesis 31.25—32.2 Titus 1
Thursday	28 February G	Ecclesiasticus 5.1–8 or James 2.1–9 Psalm 1 or 34.1–7 Mark 9.41–end	Psalm 78.1–39* 2 Chronicles 13.1—14.1 John 20.1–10	Psalm 78.40–end* Genesis 32.3–30 Titus 2
Friday	1 March Gw David, bishop, patron of Wales, c.601 (see p.79)	Ecclesiasticus 6.5–17 or James 2.14–24, 26 Psalm 119.19–24 or 112 Mark 10.1–12	Psalm 55 2 Chronicles 14.2–end John 20.11–18	Psalm 69 Genesis 33.1–17 Titus 3
Saturday	2 March Gw Chad, bishop, missionary, 672 (see p.80)	Ecclesiasticus 17.1–15 or James 3.1–10 Psalm 103.13–18 or 12.1–7 Mark 10.13–16	Psalms 76, 79 2 Chronicles 15.1–15 John 20.19–end	Psalms 81, 84 Genesis 35 Philemon

Sunday next before Lent

		Principal Service	3rd Service	2nd Service
Sunday	**3 March** G Sunday next before Lent	Exodus 34.29–end Psalm 99 2 Corinthians 3.12—4.2 Luke 9.28–36 [37–43a]	Psalm 2 Exodus 33.17–end 1 John 3.1–3	Psalm 89.1–18 [or 89.5–12] Exodus 3.1–6 John 12.27–36a

		Holy Communion	Morning Prayer	Evening Prayer
Monday	**4 March** G DEL week 8	Ecclesiasticus 17.24–29 or James 3.13–end Psalm 32.1–8 or 19.7–end Mark 10.17–27	Psalms **80**, 82 Jeremiah 1 John 3.1–21	Psalms **85**, 86 Genesis 37.1–11 Galatians 1
Tuesday	**5 March** G	Ecclesiasticus 35.1–12 or James 4.1–10 Psalm 50.1–6 or 55.7–9, 24 Mark 10.28–31	Psalms 87, **89.1–18** Jeremiah 2.1–13 John 3.22–end	Psalm **89.19–end** Genesis 37.12–end Galatians 2.1–10

		Principal Service	3rd Service	2nd Service
Wednesday	**6 March** P(La) **Ash Wednesday**	Joel 2.1–2, 12–17 or Isaiah 58.1–12 Psalm 51.1–18 2 Corinthians 5.20b—6.10 Matthew 6.1–6, 16–21 or John 8.1–11	MP Psalm 38 Daniel 9.3–6, 17–19 1 Timothy 6.6–19	EP Psalm **51** or 102 [or 102.1–18] Isaiah 1.10–18 Luke 15.11–end

		Holy Communion	Morning Prayer	Evening Prayer
Thursday	**7 March** P(La)r Perpetua, Felicity and companions, martyrs, 203 (see p.77)	Deuteronomy 30.15–end Psalm 1 Luke 9.22–25	Psalm **77** or 90, **92** Jeremiah 2.14–32 John 4.1–26	Psalm **74** or **94** Genesis 39 Galatians 2.11–end
Friday	**8 March** P(La)w Edward King, bishop, 1910 (see p.79) Felix, bishop, 647 Geoffrey Studdert Kennedy, priest, poet, 1929	Isaiah 58.1–9a Psalm 51.1–5, 17–18 Matthew 9.14–15	Psalms **3**, 7 or **88** (95) Jeremiah 3.6–22 John 4.27–42	Psalm **31** or **102** Genesis 40 Galatians 3.1–14
Saturday	**9 March** P(La)	Isaiah 58.9b–end Psalm 86.1–7 Luke 5.27–32	Psalm **71** or 96, **97**, 100 Jeremiah 4.1–18 John 4.43–end	Psalm **73** or **104** Genesis 41.1–24 Galatians 3.15–22

Lent 1

			Principal Service	3rd Service	2nd Service
Sunday	10 March 1st Sunday of Lent	P(La)	Deuteronomy 26.1–11 Psalm 91.1, 2, 9–end [or 91.1–11] Romans 10.8b–13 Luke 4.1–13	Psalm 50.1–15 Micah 6.1–8 Luke 5.27–end	Psalm 119.73–88 Jonah 3 Luke 18.9–14
			Holy Communion	Morning Prayer	Evening Prayer
Monday	11 March	P(La)	Leviticus 19.1–2, 11–18 Psalm 19.7–end Matthew 25.31–end	Psalms 10, 11 or 98, 99, 101 Jeremiah 4.19–end John 5.1–18	Psalms 12, 13, 14 or 105* (or 103) Genesis 41.25–45 Galatians 3.23—4.7
Tuesday	12 March	P(La)	Isaiah 55.10–11 Psalm 34.4–6, 21–22 Matthew 6.7–15	Psalm 44 or 106* (or 103) Jeremiah 5.1–19 John 5.19–29	Psalms 46, 49 or 107* Genesis 41.46—42.5 Galatians 4.8–20
Wednesday	13 March Ember Day	P(La)	Jonah 3 Psalm 51.1–5, 17–18 Luke 11.29–32	Psalms 6, 17 or 110, 111, 112 Jeremiah 5.20–end John 5.30–end	Psalms 9, 28 or 119.129–152 Genesis 42.6–17 Galatians 4.21—5.1
Thursday	14 March	P(La)	Esther 14.1–5, 12–14 or Isaiah 55.6–9 Psalm 138 Matthew 7.7–12	Psalms 42, 43 or 113, 115 Jeremiah 6.9–21 John 6.1–15	Psalms 137, 138, 142 or 114, 116, 117 Genesis 42.18–28 Galatians 5.2–15
Friday	15 March Ember Day	P(La)	Ezekiel 18.21–28 Psalm 130 Matthew 5.20–26	Psalm 22 or 139 Jeremiah 6.22–end John 6.16–27	Psalms 54, 55 or 130, 131, 137 Genesis 42.29–end Galatians 5.16–end
Saturday	16 March Ember Day	P(La)	Deuteronomy 26.16–end Psalm 119.1–8 Matthew 5.43–end	Psalm 59, 63 or 120, 121, 122 Jeremiah 7.1–20 John 6.27–40	Psalms 4, 16 or 118 Genesis 43.1–15 Galatians 6

Lent 2

		Principal Service	3rd Service	2nd Service
Sunday	**17 March** P(La) **2nd Sunday of Lent**	Genesis 15.1–12, 17–18 Psalm 27 Philippians 3.17—4.1 Luke 13.31–end	Psalm 119.161–end Genesis 17.1–7, 15–16 Romans 11.13–24	Psalm 135 [or 135.1–14] Jeremiah 22.1–9, 13–17 Luke 14.27–33
		Holy Communion	**Morning Prayer**	**Evening Prayer**
Monday	**18 March** P(La) *Cyril, bishop, teacher of the faith, 386*	Daniel 9.4–10 Psalm 79.8–9, 12, 14 Luke 6.36–38	Psalms 26, 32 or 123, 124, 125, 126 Jeremiah 7.21–end John 6.41–51	Psalms 70, 74 or 127, 128, 129 Genesis 43.16–end Hebrews 1 *or:* 1st EP of Joseph of Nazareth: Psalm 132; Hosea 11.1–9; Luke 2.41–end
		Principal Service	**3rd Service**	**2nd Service**
Tuesday	**19 March** W Joseph of Nazareth	2 Samuel 7.4–16 Psalm 89.26–36 Romans 4.13–18 Matthew 1.18–end	MP Psalms 25, 147.1–12 Isaiah 11.1–10 Matthew 13.54–end	EP Psalms 1, 112 Genesis 50.22–end Matthew 2.13–end
		Holy Communion	**Morning Prayer**	**Evening Prayer**
Wednesday	**20 March** P(La)w *Cuthbert, bishop, missionary, 687 (see p.80)*	Jeremiah 18.18–20 Psalm 31.4–5, 14–18 Matthew 20.17–28	Psalm 35 or 119.153–end Jeremiah 8.18—9.11 John 6.60–end	Psalms 3, 51 or 136 Genesis 44.18–end Hebrews 2.10–end
Thursday	**21 March** P(La)r *Thomas Cranmer, archbishop, Reformation martyr, 1556 (see p.77)*	Jeremiah 17.5–10 Psalm 1 Luke 16.19–end	Psalm 34 or 143, 146 Jeremiah 9.12–24 John 7.1–13	Psalm 71 or 138, 140, 141 Genesis 45.1–15 Hebrews 3.1–6
Friday	**22 March** P(La)	Genesis 37.3–4, 12–13, 17–28 Psalm 105.16–22 Matthew 21.33–43, 45–46	Psalms 40, 41 or 142, 144 Jeremiah 10.1–16 John 7.14–24	Psalms 6, 38 or 145 Genesis 45.16–end Hebrews 3.7–end
Saturday	**23 March** P(La)	Micah 7.14–15, 18–20 Psalm 103.1–4, 9–12 Luke 15.1–3, 11–end	Psalms 3, 25 or 147 Jeremiah 10.17–24 John 7.25–36	Psalms 23, 27 or 148, 149, 150 Genesis 46.1–7, 28–end Hebrews 4.1–13

Lent 3

			Principal Service	3rd Service	2nd Service
Sunday	24 March 3rd Sunday of Lent	P(La)	Isaiah 55.1–9 Psalm 63.1–9 1 Corinthians 10.1–13 Luke 13.1–9	Psalms 26, 28 Deuteronomy 6.4–9 John 17.1a, 11b–19	Psalms 12, 13 Genesis 28.10–19a John 1.35–end or: **1st EP of the Annunciation** Psalm 85; Wisdom 9.1–12 or Genesis 3.8–15; Galatians 4.1–5
Monday	25 March **Annunciation of Our Lord to the Blessed Virgin Mary**	Gold or W	Isaiah 7.10–14 Psalm 40.5–11 Hebrews 10.4–10 Luke 1.26–38	MP Psalms 111, 113 1 Samuel 2.1–10 Romans 5.12–end	EP Psalms 131, 146 Isaiah 52.1–12 Hebrews 2.5–end

The following readings may replace those provided for Holy Communion on any day during the Third Week of Lent (except the Feast of the Annunciation):
Exodus 17.1–7; Psalm 95.1–2, 6–end; John 4.5–42

			Holy Communion	Morning Prayer	Evening Prayer
Tuesday	26 March Harriet Monsell, founder of the Community of St John the Baptist, 1883	P(La)	Song of the Three 2, 11–20 or Daniel 2.20–23 Psalm 25.3–10 Matthew 18.21–end	Psalms 6, **9** or **5**, 6 (8) Jeremiah 11.18—12.6 John 7.53—8.11	Psalms 61, 62, **64** or **9**, 10* Genesis 47.28—end of 48 Hebrews 5.11—6.12
Wednesday	27 March	P(La)	Deuteronomy 4.1, 5–9 Psalm 147.13–end Matthew 5.17–19	Psalm **38**, **39** or **11**, 12, 13 Jeremiah 13.1—11 John 8.12–30	Psalms 36, **39** or **11**, 12, 13 Genesis 49.1–32 Hebrews 6.13–end
Thursday	28 March	P(La)	Jeremiah 7.23–28 Psalm 95.1–2, 6–end Luke 11.14–23	Psalms **56**, 57 or 14, **15**, 16 Jeremiah 14 John 8.31–47	Psalms **59**, 60 or **18*** Genesis 49.33—end of 50 Hebrews 7.1–10
Friday	29 March	P(La)	Hosea 14 Psalm 81.6–10, 13, 16 Mark 12.28–34	Psalm **22** or 17, **19** Jeremiah 15.10–end John 8.48–end	Psalm **69** or **22** Exodus 1.1–14 Hebrews 7.11–end
Saturday	30 March	P(La)	Hosea 5.15—6.6 Psalm 51.1–2, 17–end Luke 18.9–14	Psalm **31** or 20, 21, **23** Jeremiah 16.10—17.4 John 9.1–17	Psalms **116**, 130 or **24**, 25 Exodus 1.22—2.10 Hebrews 8

Lent 4

		Principal Service	3rd Service	2nd Service
Sunday	**31 March** *P(La)* **4th Sunday of Lent**	Joshua 5.9–12 Psalm 32 2 Corinthians 5.16–end Luke 15.1–3,11b–end	Psalms 84, 85 Genesis 37.3–4, 12–end 1 Peter 2.16–end	Psalm 30 Prayer of Manasseh or Isaiah 40.27—41.13 2 Timothy 4.1–18 HC John 11.17-44

For Mothering Sunday:
Exodus 2.1–10 or 1 Samuel 1.20–end; Psalm 34.11–20 or 127.1–4;
2 Corinthians 1.3–7 or Colossians 3.12–17; Luke 2.33–35 or John 19.25b–27
If the Principal Service readings have been displaced by Mothering Sunday provisions, they may be used at the Second Service.

		Holy Communion	Morning Prayer	Evening Prayer
		The following readings may replace those provided for Holy Communion on any day during the Fourth Week of Lent: Micah 7.7–9; Psalm 27.1, 9–10, 16–17; John 9		
Monday	**1 April** *P(La)* Frederick Denison Maurice, priest, teacher of the faith, 1872	Isaiah 65.17–21 Psalm 30.1–5, 8, 11–end John 4.43–end	Psalms 70, **77** or 27, **30** Jeremiah 17.5–18 John 9.18–end	Psalms **25**, 28 or 26, **28, 29** Exodus 2.11–22 Hebrews 9.1–14
Tuesday	**2 April** *P(La)*	Ezekiel 47.1–9, 12 Psalm 46.1–8 John 5.1–3, 5–16	Psalms 54, **79** or 32, **36** Jeremiah 18.1–12 John 10.1–10	Psalms 80, 82 or **33** Exodus 2.23—3.20 Hebrews 9.15–end
Wednesday	**3 April** *P(La)*	Isaiah 49.8–15 Psalm 145.8–18 John 5.17–30	Psalms 63, **90** or **34** Jeremiah 18.13–end John 10.11–21	Psalms 52, **91** or **119.33–56** Exodus 4.1–23 Hebrews 10.1–18
Thursday	**4 April** *P(La)*	Exodus 32.7–14 Psalm 106.19–23 John 5.31–end	Psalms 53, **86** or **37*** Jeremiah 19.1–13 John 10.22–end	Psalm **94** or 39, **40** Exodus 4.27—6.1 Hebrews 10.19–25
Friday	**5 April** *P(La)*	Wisdom 2.1, 12–22 or Jeremiah 26.8–11 Psalm 34.15–end John 7.1–2, 10, 25–30	Psalm **102** or **31** Jeremiah 19.14—20.6 John 11.1–16	Psalms 13, **16** or **35** Exodus 6.2–13 Hebrews 10.26–end
Saturday	**6 April** *P(La)*	Jeremiah 11.18–20 Psalm 7.1–2, 8–10 John 7.40–52	Psalm **32** or 41, **42**, 43 Jeremiah 20.7–end John 11.17–27	Psalms **140**, 141, 142 or 45, **46** Exodus 7.8–end Hebrews 11.1–16

Lent 5

		Principal Service	3rd Service	2nd Service
Sunday	**7 April** P(La) **5th Sunday of Lent** *Passiontide begins*	Isaiah 43.16–21 Psalm 126 Philippians 3.4b–14 John 12.1–8	Psalms 111, 112 Isaiah 35 Romans 7.21—8.4	Psalm 35 [or 35.1–9] 2 Chronicles 35.1–6, 10–16 Luke 22.1–13

The following readings may replace those provided for Holy Communion on any day during the Fifth Week of Lent:
2 Kings 4.18–21, 32–37; Psalm 17.1–8, 16; John 11.1–45

		Holy Communion	Morning Prayer	Evening Prayer
Monday	**8 April** P(La)	Susanna 1–9, 15–17, 19–30, 33–62 [or 41b–62] or Joshua 2.1–14 Psalm 23 John 8.1–11	Psalms **73**, 121 or **44** Jeremiah 21.1–10 John 11.28–44	Psalms **26**, 27 or **47**, 49 Exodus 8.1–19 Hebrews 11.17–31
Tuesday	**9 April** P(La) Dietrich Bonhoeffer, Lutheran pastor, martyr, 1945	Numbers 21.4–9 Psalm 102.1–3, 16–23 John 8.21–30	Psalms **35**, 123 or **48**, 52 Jeremiah 22.1–5, 13–19 John 11.45–end	Psalms **61**, 64 or **50** Exodus 8.20–end Hebrews 11.32—12.2
Wednesday	**10 April** P(La)w William Law, priest, spiritual writer, 1761 (see p.78) William of Ockham, friar, philosopher, teacher of the faith, 1347	Daniel 3.14–20, 24–25, 28 Canticle: Bless the Lord John 8.31–42	Psalms **55**, 124 or 11**9**.57–80 Jeremiah 22.20—23.8 John 12.1–11	Psalms 56, **62** or **59**, 60 (67) Exodus 9.1–12 Hebrews 12.3–13
Thursday	**11 April** P(La) George Selwyn, bishop, 1878	Genesis 17.3–9 Psalm 105.4–9 John 8.51–end	Psalms **40**, 125 or 56, **57** (63*) Jeremiah 23.9–32 John 12.12–19	Psalms 42, **43** or 61, **62**, 64 Exodus 9.13–end Hebrews 12.14–end
Friday	**12 April** P(La)	Jeremiah 20.10–13 Psalm 18.1–6 John 10.31–end	Psalms **22**, 126 or **51**, 54 Jeremiah 24 John 12.20–36a	Psalm **31** or **38** Exodus 10 Hebrews 13.1–16
Saturday	**13 April** P(La)	Ezekiel 37.21–end Canticle: Jeremiah 31.10–13 or Psalm 121 John 11.45–end	Psalms **23**, 127 or **68** Jeremiah 25.1–14 John 12.36b–end	Psalms 128, 129, **130** or 65, **66** Exodus 11 Hebrews 13.17–end

Holy Week

		Principal Service		3rd Service	2nd Service
Sunday	**14 April** **Palm Sunday** R	Liturgy of the Palms: Luke 19.28–40 Psalm 118.1–2, 19–end [or 118.19–24]	Liturgy of the Passion: Isaiah 50.4–9a Psalm 31.9–16 [or 31.9–18] Philippians 2.5–11 Luke 22.14—end of 23 or Luke 23.1–49	Psalms 61, 62 Zechariah 9.9–12 1 Corinthians 2.1–12	Psalm 69.1–20 Isaiah 5.1–7 Luke 20.9–19

		Holy Communion	Morning Prayer	Evening Prayer

From the Monday of Holy Week until the Saturday of Easter Week the seasonal psalmody must be used.

		Holy Communion	Morning Prayer	Evening Prayer
Monday	**15 April** Monday of Holy Week R	Isaiah 42.1–9 Psalm 36.5–11 Hebrews 9.11–15 John 12.1–11	Psalm 41 Lamentations 1.1–12a Luke 22.1–23	Psalm 25 Lamentations 2.8–19 Colossians 1.18–23
Tuesday	**16 April** Tuesday of Holy Week R	Isaiah 49.1–7 Psalm 71.1–14 [or 71.1–8] 1 Corinthians 1.18–31 John 12.20–36	Psalm 27 Lamentations 3.1–18 Luke 22. [24–38] 39–53	Psalm 55.13–24 Lamentations 3.40–51 Galatians 6.11–end
Wednesday	**17 April** Wednesday of Holy Week R	Isaiah 50.4–9a Psalm 70 Hebrews 12.1–3 John 13.21–32	Psalm 102 [or 102.1–18] Wisdom 1.16—2.1; 2.12–22 or Jeremiah 11.18–20 Luke 22.54–end	Psalm 88 Isaiah 63.1–9 Revelation 14.18—15.4
Thursday	**18 April** **Maundy Thursday** W	Exodus 12.1–4 [5–10] 11–14 Psalm 116.1, 10–end [or 116.9–end] 1 Corinthians 11.23–26 John 13.1–17, 31b–35	Psalms 42, 43 Leviticus 16.2–24 Luke 23.1–25	Psalm 39 Exodus 11 Ephesians 2.11–18
Friday	**19 April** **Good Friday** Hangings removed; R for the Liturgy	Isaiah 52.13—end of 53 Psalm 22 [or 22.1–11 or 22.1–21] Hebrews 10.16–25 or Hebrews 4.14–16; 5.7–9 John 18.1—end of 19	Psalm 69 Genesis 22.1–18 A part of John 18 and 19 may be read, if not used at the Principal Service or Hebrews 10.1–10	Psalms 130, 143 Lamentations 5.15–end John 19.38–end or Colossians 1.18–23

Easter

		Principal Service	3rd Service	2nd Service
Saturday	**20 April** **Easter Eve** *Hangings removed* *These readings are for use at services other than the Easter Vigil.*	Job 14.1–14 or Lamentations 3.1–9, 19–24 Psalm 31.1–4, 15–16 [or 31.1–5] 1 Peter 4.1–8 Matthew 27.57–end or John 19.38–end	Psalm 142 Hosea 6.1–6 John 2.18–22	Psalm 116 Job 19.21–27 1 John 5.5–12
Saturday *or Sunday*	**20 April evening** **21 April morning** *Gold or W* *Easter Vigil* *The New Testament readings should be preceded by a minimum of three Old Testament readings.* *The Exodus reading should always be used.*	Genesis 1.1—2.4a Genesis 7.1–5, 11–18; 8.6–18; 9.8–13 Genesis 22.1–18 **Exodus 14.10–end; 15.20–21** Isaiah 55.1–11 Baruch 3.9–15, 32—4.4 or Proverbs 8.1–8, 19–21; 9.4b–6 Ezekiel 36.24–28 Ezekiel 37.1–14 Zephaniah 3.14–end **Romans 6.3–11** **Luke 24.1–12**	Psalm 136.1–9, 23–end Psalm 46 Psalm 16 **Canticle: Exodus 15.1b–13, 17–18** *Canticle:* Isaiah 12.2–end Psalm 19 Psalms 42, 43 Psalm 143 Psalm 98 **Psalm 114**	
Sunday	**21 April** **Easter Day** *Gold or W*	Acts 10.34–43 † or Isaiah 65.17–end Psalm 118.1–2, 14–24 [or 118.14–24] 1 Corinthians 15.19–26 or Acts 10.34–43† John 20.1–18 or Luke 24.1–12 † *The reading from Acts must be used as either the first or second reading.*	MP Psalms 114, 117 Ezekiel 47.1–12 John 2.13–22	EP Psalms 105 or 66.1–11 Isaiah 43.1–21 1 Corinthians 15.1–11 or John 20.19–23

Easter Week

		Holy Communion	Morning Prayer	Evening Prayer
Monday	**22 April** W Monday of Easter Week	Acts 2.14, 22–32 Psalm 16.1–2, 6–end Matthew 28.8–15	Psalms **111**, 117, 146 Song of Solomon 1.9—2.7 Mark 16.1–8	Psalm **135** Exodus 12.1–14 1 Corinthians 15.1–11
Tuesday	**23 April** W Tuesday of Easter Week	Acts 2.36–41 Psalm 33.4–5, 18–end John 20.11–18	Psalms **112**, 147.1–12 Song of Solomon 2.8–end Luke 24.1–12	Psalm **136** Exodus 12.14–36 1 Corinthians 15.12–19
Wednesday	**24 April** W Wednesday of Easter Week	Acts 3.1–10 Psalm 105.1–9 Luke 24.13–35	Psalms **113**, 147.13–end Song of Solomon 3 Matthew 28.16–end	Psalm **105** Exodus 12.37–end 1 Corinthians 15.20–28
Thursday	**25 April** W Thursday of Easter Week	Acts 3.11–end Psalm 8 Luke 24.35–48	Psalms **114**, 148 Song of Solomon 5.2—6.3 Luke 7.11–17	Psalm **106** Exodus 13.1–16 1 Corinthians 15.29–34
Friday	**26 April** W Friday of Easter Week	Acts 4.1–12 Psalm 118.1–4, 22–26 John 21.1–14	Psalms **115**, 149 Song of Solomon 7.10—8.4 Luke 8.41–end	Psalm **107** Exodus 13.17—14.14 1 Corinthians 15.35–50
Saturday	**27 April** W Saturday of Easter Week	Acts 4.13–21 Psalm 118.1–4, 14–21 Mark 16.9–15	Psalms **116**, 150 Song of Solomon 8.5–7 John 11.17–44	Psalm **145** Exodus 14.15–end 1 Corinthians 15.51–end

Easter 2

		Principal Service	3rd Service	2nd Service
Sunday	**28 April** W 2nd Sunday of Easter	[Exodus 14.10–end; 15.20–21] Acts 5.27–32† Psalm 118.14–end or Psalm 150 Revelation 1.4–8 John 20.19–end † The reading from Acts must be used as either the first or second reading.	Psalm 136.1–16 Exodus 12.1 Psalm13 1 Peter 1.3–12	Psalm 16 Isaiah 52.13—53.12 or 53.1–6, 9–12 Luke 24.13–35 or: 1st EP of George, martyr, patron of England: Psalms 111, 116; Jeremiah 15.15–end; Hebrews 11.32—12.2
Monday	**29 April** R George, martyr, patron of England, c.304 (transferred from 23 April)	1 Maccabees 2.59–64 or Revelation 12.7–12 Psalm 126 2 Timothy 2.3–13 John 15.18–21	MP Psalms 5, 146 Joshua 1.1–9 Ephesians 6.10–20	EP Psalms 3, 11 Isaiah 43.1–7 John 15.1–8 or: 1st EP of Mark the Evangelist: Psalm 19; Isaiah 52.7–10; Mark 1.1–15
Tuesday	**30 April** R Mark the Evangelist (transferred from 25 April)	Proverbs 15.28–end or Acts 15.35–end Psalm 119.9–16 Ephesians 4.7–16 Mark 13.5–13	MP Psalms 37.23–end, 148 Isaiah 62.6–10 or Ecclesiasticus 51.13–end Acts 12.25—13.13	EP Psalm 45 Ezekiel 1.4–14 2 Timothy 4.1–11 or: 1st EP of Philip and James, Apostles: Psalm 25; Isaiah 40.27–end; John 12.20–26
Wednesday	**1 May** R Philip and James, Apostles	Isaiah 30.15–21 Psalm 119.1–8 Ephesians 1.3–10 John 14.1–14	MP Psalms 139, 146 Proverbs 4.10–18 James 1.1–12	EP Psalm 149 Job 23.1–12 John 1.43–end
		Holy Communion	Morning Prayer	Evening Prayer
Thursday	**2 May** W Athanasius, bishop, teacher of the faith, 373 (see p.78)	Acts 5.27–33 Psalm 34.1, 15–end John 3.31–end	Psalms 28, 29 or 14, **15**, 16 Deuteronomy 4.1–14 John 21.1–14	Psalm **34** or **18*** Exodus 17 Colossians 2.16—3.11
Friday	**3 May** W	Acts 5.34–42 Psalm 27.1–5, 16–17 John 6.1–15	Psalms 57, **61** or 17, **19** Deuteronomy 4.15–31 John 21.15–19	Psalm **118** or **22** Exodus 18.1–12 Colossians 3.12—4.1
Saturday	**4 May** W English saints and martyrs of the Reformation Era	Acts 6.1–7 Psalm 33.1–5, 18–19 John 6.16–21 *Lesser Festival eucharistic lectionary:* Isaiah 43.1–7 or Ecclesiasticus 2.10–17 Psalm 87 2 Corinthians 4.5–12 John 12.20–26	Psalms 63, **84** or 20, 21, **23** Deuteronomy 4.32–40 John 21.20–end	Psalm **66** or **24**, 25 Exodus 18.13–end Colossians 4.2–end

Easter 3

		Principal Service	3rd Service	2nd Service
Sunday	**5 May** **3rd Sunday of Easter** W	[Zephaniah 3.14–end] Acts 9.1–6 [7–20]† Psalm 30 Revelation 5.11–end John 21.1–19 † The reading from Acts must be used as either the first or second reading.	Psalm 80.1–8 Exodus 15.1–2, 9–18 John 10.1–19	Psalm 86 Isaiah 38.9–20 John 11.[17–26] 27–44

		Holy Communion	Morning Prayer	Evening Prayer
Monday	**6 May** W	Acts 6.8–15 Psalm 119.17–24 John 6.22–29	Psalms **96**, 97 or 27, **30** Deuteronomy 5.1–22 Ephesians 1.1–14	Psalm **61**, 65 or 26, **28**, 29 Exodus 19 Luke 1.1–25
Tuesday	**7 May** W	Acts 7.51—8.1a Psalm 31.1–5, 16 John 6.30–35	Psalms **98**, 99, 100 or 32, **36** Deuteronomy 5.22–end Ephesians 1.15–end	Psalm **71** or **33** Exodus 20.1–21 Luke 1.26–38
Wednesday	**8 May** W Julian of Norwich, spiritual writer, c.1417 (see p.80)	Acts 8.1b–8 Psalm 66.1–6 John 6.35–40	Psalm **105** or **34** Deuteronomy 6 Ephesians 2.1–10	Psalms 67, **72** or 1**19.33–56** Exodus 24 Luke 1.39–56
Thursday	**9 May** W	Acts 8.26–end Psalm 66.7–8, 14–end John 6.44–51	Psalm **136** or **37*** Deuteronomy 7.1–11 Ephesians 2.11–end	Psalm **73** or 39, **40** Exodus 25.1–22 Luke 1.57–end
Friday	**10 May** W	Acts 9.1–20 Psalm 117 John 6.52–59	Psalm **107** or **31** Deuteronomy 7.12–end Ephesians 3.1–13	Psalm **77** or **35** Exodus 28.1–4a, 29–38 Luke 2.1–20
Saturday	**11 May** W	Acts 9.31–42 Psalm 116.10–15 John 6.60–69	Psalms 108, **110**, 111 or 41, **42**, 43 Deuteronomy 8 Ephesians 3.14–end	Psalms 23, **27** or 45, **46** Exodus 29.1–9 Luke 2.21–40

Easter 4

Sunday 12 May — 4th Sunday of Easter — W

Principal Service
[Genesis 7.1–5, 11–18; 8.6–18; 9.8–13]
Acts 9.36–end†
Psalm 23
Revelation 7.9–end
John 10.22–30
† The reading from Acts must be used as either the first or second reading.

3rd Service
Psalm 146
1 Kings 17.17–end
Luke 7.11–23

2nd Service
Psalms 113, 114
Isaiah 63.7–14
Luke 24.36–49

Monday 13 May — W

Holy Communion
Acts 11.1–18
Psalms 42.1–2; 43.1–4
John 10.1–10 (or 11–18)

Morning Prayer
Psalm **103** or **44**
Deuteronomy 9.1–21
Ephesians 4.1–16

Evening Prayer
Psalms 112, 113, **114** or **47**, **49**
Exodus 32.1–14
Luke 2.41–end
or: 1st EP of Matthias the Apostle:
Psalm 147; Isaiah 22.15–22
Philippians 3.13b–4.1

Tuesday 14 May — Matthias the Apostle — R

Principal Service
Isaiah 22.15–end
or Acts 1.15–end
Psalm 15
Acts 1.15–end
or 1 Corinthians 4.1–7
John 15.9–17

3rd Service
MP Psalms 16, 147.1–12
1 Samuel 2.27–35
Acts 2.37–end

2nd Service
EP Psalm 80
1 Samuel 16.1–13a
Matthew 7.15–27

Wednesday 15 May — W

Holy Communion
Acts 12.24—13.5
Psalm 67
John 12.44–end

Morning Prayer
Psalm **135**, or **119.57–80**
Deuteronomy 10.12–end
Ephesians 5.1–14

Evening Prayer
Psalms **47**, 48 or **59**, 60 (67)
Exodus 33
Luke 3.15–22

Thursday 16 May — Caroline Chisholm, social reformer, 1877 — W

Holy Communion
Acts 13.13–25
Psalm 89.1–2, 20–26
John 13.16–20

Morning Prayer
Psalm **118** or 56, **57** (63*)
Deuteronomy 11.8–end
Ephesians 5.15–end

Evening Prayer
Psalms 81, **85** or 61, **62**, 64
Exodus 34.1–10, 27–end
Luke 4.1–13

Friday 17 May — W

Holy Communion
Acts 13.26–33
Psalm 2
John 14.1–6

Morning Prayer
Psalm **33** or **51**, 54
Deuteronomy 12.1–14
Ephesians 6.1–9

Evening Prayer
Psalms **36**, 40 or **38**
Exodus 35.20—36.7
Luke 4.14–30

Saturday 18 May — W

Holy Communion
Acts 13.44–end
Psalm 98.1–5
John 14.7–14

Morning Prayer
Psalm **34** or **68**
Deuteronomy 15.1–18
Ephesians 6.10–end

Evening Prayer
Psalms **84**, 86 or 65, **66**
Exodus 40.17–end
Luke 4.31–37

Easter 5

		Principal Service	3rd Service	2nd Service
Sunday	19 May W 5th Sunday of Easter	[Baruch 3.9–15, 32—4.4 or Genesis 22.1–18] Acts 11.1–18† Psalm 148 [or 148.1–6] Revelation 21.1–6 John 13.31–35 † *The reading from Acts must be used as either the first or second reading.*	Psalm 16 2 Samuel 7.4–13 Acts 2.14a, 22–32 [33–36]	Psalm 98 Daniel 6. [1–5] 6–23 Mark 15.46—16.8

		Holy Communion	Morning Prayer	Evening Prayer
Monday	20 May W Alcuin, deacon, abbot, 804 (see p.80)	Acts 14.5–18 Psalm 118.1–3, 14–15 John 14.21–26	Psalm 145 or 71 Deuteronomy 16.1–20 1 Peter 1.1–12	Psalm 105 or 72, 75 Numbers 9.15–end; 10.33–end Luke 4.38–end
Tuesday	21 May W *Helena, protector of the Holy Places, 330*	Acts 14.19–end Psalm 145.10–end John 14.27–end	Psalms 19, 147.1–12 or 73 Deuteronomy 17.8–end 1 Peter 1.13–end	Psalms 96, 97 or 74 Numbers 11.1–33 Luke 5.1–11
Wednesday	22 May W	Acts 15.1–6 Psalm 122.1–5 John 15.1–8	Psalms 30, 147.13–end or 77 Deuteronomy 18.9–end 1 Peter 2.1–10	Psalms 98, 99, 100 or 119.81–104 Numbers 12 Luke 5.12–26
Thursday	23 May W	Acts 15.7–21 Psalm 96.1–3, 7–10 John 15.9–11	Psalms 57, 148 or 78.1–39* Deuteronomy 19 1 Peter 2.11–end	Psalm 104 or 78.40–end* Numbers 13.1–3, 17–end Luke 5.27–end
Friday	24 May W John and Charles Wesley, evangelists, hymn writers, 1791 and 1788 (see p.79)	Acts 15.22–31 Psalm 57.8–end John 15.12–17	Psalms 138, 149 or 55 Deuteronomy 21.22—22.8 1 Peter 3.1–12	Psalm 66 or 69 Numbers 14.1–25 Luke 6.1–11
Saturday	25 May W The Venerable Bede, monk, scholar, historian, 735 (see p.80) *Aldhelm, bishop, 709*	Acts 16.1–10 Psalm 100 John 15.18–21	Psalms 146, 150 or 76, 79 Deuteronomy 24.5–end 1 Peter 3.13–end	Psalm 118 or 81, 84 Numbers 14.26–end Luke 6.12–26

35

Easter 6

		Principal Service	3rd Service	2nd Service
Sunday	26 May W 6th Sunday of Easter	[Ezekiel 37.1–14] Acts 16.9–15† Psalm 67 Revelation 21.10, 22—22.5 John 14.23–29 or John 5.1–9 † The reading from Acts must be used as either the first or second reading.	Psalm 40.1–9 Genesis 1.26–28 [29–end] Colossians 3.1–11	Psalms 126, 127 Zephaniah 3.14–end Matthew 28.1–10, 16–end

		Holy Communion	Morning Prayer	Evening Prayer
Monday	27 May W Rogation Day	Acts 16.11–15 Psalm 149.1–5 John 15.26—16.4	Psalms 65, 67 or 80, 82 Deuteronomy 26 1 Peter 4.1–11	Psalms 121, 122, 123 or 85, 86 Numbers 16.1–35 Luke 6.27–38
Tuesday	28 May W Rogation Day *Lanfranc, monk, archbishop, scholar, 1089*	Acts 16.22–34 Psalm 138 John 16.5–11	Psalms 124, 125, 126, 127 or 87, 89.1–18 Deuteronomy 28.1–14 1 Peter 4.12–end	Psalms 128, 129, 130, 131 or 89.19–end Numbers 16.36–end Luke 6.39–end
Wednesday	29 May W Rogation Day	Acts 17.15, 22—18.1 Psalm 148.1–2, 11–end John 16.12–15	Psalms 132, 133 or 119.105–128 Deuteronomy 28.58–end 1 Peter 5	1st EP of Ascension Day: Psalms 15, 24 2 Samuel 23.1–5 Colossians 2.20—3.4

Ascension Day / Easter 6

Thursday 30 May — Ascension Day
Gold or W

Principal Service
Acts 1.1–11 †
or Daniel 7.9–14
Psalm 47
or Psalm 93
Ephesians 1.15–end
or Acts 1.1–11†
Luke 24.44–end
† *The reading from Acts must be used as either the first or second reading.*

3rd Service
MP Psalms 110, 150
Isaiah 52.7–end
Hebrews 7. [11–25] 26–end

2nd Service
EP Psalm 8
Song of the Three 29–37
or 2 Kings 2.1–15
Revelation 5
HC Matthew 28.16–end

The nine days after Ascension Day until the eve of Pentecost are observed as days of prayer and preparation for the celebration of the outpouring of the Holy Spirit. From 1–8 June, in preparation for the Day of Pentecost, an alternative sequence of daily readings for use at the one of the offices is marked with an asterisk*.

Friday 31 May — Visit of the Blessed Virgin Mary to Elizabeth
W

Holy Communion
Zephaniah 3.14–18
Psalm 113
Romans 12.9–16
Luke 1.39–49 [50–56]

3rd Service
MP Psalms 85, 150
1 Samuel 2.1–10
Mark 3.31–end

2nd Service
EP Psalms 122, 127, 128
Zechariah 2.10–end
John 3.25–30

Saturday 1 June — Justin, martyr, c.165 (see p.77)
Wr

Holy Communion
Acts 18.22–end
Psalm 47.1–2, 7–end
John 16.23–28

Morning Prayer
Psalms 21, **47** or 96, **97**, 100
Deuteronomy 30
1 John 2.7–17
**Numbers 11.16–17, 24–29; 1 Corinthians 2*

Evening Prayer
Psalms 84, **85** or **104**
Numbers 21.4–9
Luke 7.18–35

37

Easter 7

		Principal Service	3rd Service	2nd Service
Sunday	**2 June** W **7th Sunday of Easter** *Sunday after Ascension Day*	[Ezekiel 36.24–28] Acts 16.16–34† Psalm 97 Revelation 22.12–14,16,17, 20–end John 17.20–end † *The reading from Acts must be used as either the first or second reading.*	Psalm 99 Deuteronomy 34 Luke 24.44–end or Acts 1.1–8	Psalm 68 [or 68.1–13, 18–19] Isaiah 44.1–8 Ephesians 4.7–16 HC Luke 24.44–end

		Holy Communion	Morning Prayer	Evening Prayer
Monday	**3 June** W *Martyrs of Uganda, 1885–7, 1977*	Acts 19.1–8 Psalm 68.1–6 John 16.29–end	Psalms 93, 96, 97 or 98, 99, 101 Deuteronomy 31.1–13 1 John 2.18–end *Numbers 27.15–end; 1 Corinthians 3	Psalm 18 or 105* (or 103) Numbers 22.1–35 Luke 7.36–end
Tuesday	**4 June** W *Petroc, abbot, 6th cent*	Acts 20.17–27 Psalm 68.9–10, 18–19 John 17.1–11	Psalms 98, 99, 100 or 106* (or 103) Deuteronomy 31.14–29 1 John 3.1–10 *1 Samuel 10.1–10; 1 Corinthians 12.1–13	Psalm 68 or 107* Numbers 22.36—23.12 Luke 8.1–15
Wednesday	**5 June** Wr *Boniface (Wynfrith), bishop, martyr, 754 (see p.77)*	Acts 20.28–end Psalm 68.27–28, 32–end John 17.11–19	Psalms 2, 29 or 110, 111, 112 Deuteronomy 31.30—32.14 1 John 3.11–end *1 Kings 19.1–18; Matthew 3.13–end	Psalms 36, 46 or 119.129–152 Numbers 23.13–end Luke 8.16–25
Thursday	**6 June** W *Ini Kopuria, founder of the Melanesian Brotherhood, 1945*	Acts 22.30, 23.6–11 Psalm 16.1, 5–end John 17.20–end	Psalms 24, 72 or 113, 115 Deuteronomy 32.15–47 1 John 4.1–6 *Ezekiel 11.14–20; Matthew 9.35—10.20	Psalm 139 or 114, 116, 117 Numbers 24 Luke 8.26–39
Friday	**7 June** W	Acts 25.13–21 Psalm 103.1–2, 11–12, 19–20 John 21.15–19	Psalms 28, 30 or 139 Deuteronomy 33 1 John 4.7–end *Ezekiel 36.22–28; Matthew 12.22–32	Psalm 147 or 130, 131, 137 Numbers 27.12–end Luke 8.40–end
Saturday	**8 June** W *Thomas Ken, bishop, nonjuror; hymn writer, 1711 (see p.79)*	Acts 28.16–20, 30–end Psalm 11.4–end John 21.20–end	Psalms 42, 43 or 120, 121, 122 Deuteronomy 32.48–end, 34 1 John 5	1st EP of Pentecost: Psalm 48 Deuteronomy 16.9–15 John 7.37–39

*Micah 3.1–8; Ephesians 6.10–20 (at MP only)

Pentecost / Ordinary Time

		Principal Service	3rd Service	2nd Service
Sunday	**9 June** R **Pentecost** Whit Sunday	Acts 2.1–21† or Genesis 11.1–9 Psalm 104.26–36, 37b [or 104.26–end] Romans 8.14–17 or Acts 2.1–21† John 14.8–17 [25–27] † The reading from Acts must be used as either the first or second reading.	MP Psalms 36.5–10; 150 Isaiah 40.12–23 or Wisdom 9.9–17 1 Corinthians 2.6–end	EP Psalm 33.12–12 Exodus 33.7–20 2 Corinthians 3.4–end HC John 16.4b–15
		Holy Communion	**Morning Prayer**	**Evening Prayer**
Monday	**10 June** G Ordinary Time resumes today DEL week 10	2 Corinthians 1.1–7 Psalm 34.1–8 Matthew 5.1–12	Psalms 123, 124, 125, **126** 2 Chronicles 17.1–12 Romans 1.1–17	Psalms **127**, 128, 129 Joshua 1 Luke 9.18–27 or: 1st EP of Barnabas the Apostle: Psalms 1, 15; Isaiah 42.5–12; Acts 14.8–end
		Principal Service	**3rd Service**	**2nd Service**
Tuesday	**11 June** R Barnabas the Apostle	Job 29.11–16 or Acts 11.19–end Psalm 112 Acts 11.19–end or Galatians 2.1–10 John 15.12–17	MP Psalms 100, 101, 117 Jeremiah 9.23–24 Acts 4.32–end	EP Psalm 147 Ecclesiastes 12.9–end or Tobit 4.5–11 Acts 9.26–31
		Holy Communion	**Morning Prayer**	**Evening Prayer**
Wednesday	**12 June** G	2 Corinthians 3.4–11 Psalm 78.1–4 Matthew 5.17–19	Psalm **119.153–end** 2 Chronicles 18.28—end of 19 Romans 2.1–16	Psalm **136** Joshua 3 Luke 9.37–50
Thursday	**13 June** G	2 Corinthians 3.15—4.1, 3–6 Psalm 78.36–40 Matthew 5.20–26	Psalms **143**, 146 2 Chronicles 20.1–23 Romans 2.17–end	Psalms **138**, 140, 141 Joshua 4.1—5.1 Luke 9.51–end
Friday	**14 June** G Richard Baxter, puritan divine, 1691	2 Corinthians 4.7–15 Psalm 99 Matthew 5.27–32	Psalms 142, **144** 2 Chronicles 22.10—end of 23 Romans 3.1–20	Psalm **145** Joshua 5.2–end Luke 10.1–16
Saturday	**15 June** G Evelyn Underhill, spiritual writer, 1941	2 Corinthians 5.14–end Psalm 103.1–12 Matthew 5.33–37	Psalm **147** 2 Chronicles 24.1–22 Romans 3.21–end	1st **EP of Trinity Sunday**: Psalms 97, 98 Isaiah 40.12–end Mark 1.1–13

Trinity Sunday

			Principal Service	3rd Service	2nd Service
Sunday	16 June **Trinity Sunday**	Gold or W	Proverbs 8.1–4, 22–31 Psalm 8 Romans 5.1–5 John 16.12–15	MP Psalm 29 Isaiah 6.1–8 Revelation 4	EP Psalm 73.1–3, 16–end Exodus 3.1–15 John 3.1–17
			Holy Communion	**Morning Prayer**	**Evening Prayer**
Monday	17 June *Samuel and Henrietta Barnett, social reformers, 1913 and 1936* DEL week 11	G	2 Corinthians 6.1–10 Psalm 98 Matthew 5.38–42	Psalms 1, 2, 3 2 Chronicles 26.1–21 Romans 4.1–12	Psalms **4**, 7 Joshua 7.1–15 Luke 10.25–37
Tuesday	18 June *Bernard Mizeki, martyr, 1896*	G	2 Corinthians 8.1–9 Psalm 146 Matthew 5.43–end	Psalms **5**, 6 (8) 2 Chronicles 28 Romans 4.13–end	Psalms **9**, 10* Joshua 7.16–end Luke 10.38–end
Wednesday	19 June *Sundar Singh, sadhu (holy man), evangelist, teacher of the faith, 1929*	G	2 Corinthians 9.6–11 Psalm 112 Matthew 6.1–6, 16–18	Psalm **119.1–32** 2 Chronicles 29.1–19 Romans 5.1–11	Psalms **11**, 12, 13 Joshua 8.1–29 Luke 11.1–13 *or:* 1st EP of Corpus Christi: Psalms 110, 111; Exodus 16.2–15; John 6.22–35
			Principal Service	**3rd Service**	**2nd Service**
Thursday	20 June Day of Thanksgiving for the Institution of Holy Communion (Corpus Christi)	W	Genesis 14.18–20 Psalm 116.10–end 1 Corinthians 11.23–26 John 6.51–58	MP Psalm 147 Deuteronomy 8.2–16 1 Corinthians 10.1–17	EP Psalms 23, 42, 43 Proverbs 9.1–5 Luke 9.11–17
	Alternatively Corpus Christi may be kept as a Lesser Festival, and either these readings or those given below may be used.				
			Holy Communion	**Morning Prayer**	**Evening Prayer**
or Thursday	20 June Day of Thanksgiving for the Institution of the Holy Communion (Corpus Christi)	Gw	2 Corinthians 11.1–11 Psalm 111 Matthew 6.7–15	Psalms 14, **15**, 16 2 Chronicles 29.20–end Romans 5.12–end	Psalm **18*** Joshua 8.30–end Luke 11.14–28
Friday	21 June	G	2 Corinthians 11.18, 21b–30 Psalm 34.1–6 Matthew 6.19–23	Psalms 17, **19** 2 Chronicles 30 Romans 6.1–14	Psalm **22** Joshua 9.3–36 Luke 11.29–36
Saturday	22 June *Alban, first martyr of Britain, c.250 (see p.77)*	Gr	2 Corinthians 12.1–10 Psalm 89.20–33 Matthew 6.24–end	Psalms 20, 21, **23** 2 Chronicles 32.1–22 Romans 6.15–end	Psalms **24**, 25 Joshua 10.1–15 Luke 11.37–end

Trinity 1

Sunday 23 June — G
1st Sunday after Trinity
Proper 7

Principal Service
Continuous:
1 Kings 19.1–4 [5–7] 8–15a
Psalms 42, 43 [or 42 or 43]
Galatians 3.23–end
Luke 8.26–39

Related:
Isaiah 65.1–9
Psalm 22.19–28

3rd Service
Psalm 55.1–16,18–21
Deuteronomy 11.1–15
Acts 27.1–12

2nd Service
Psalms [50] 57
Genesis 24.1–27
Mark 5.21–end
or: 1st EP of the Birth of John the Baptist:
Psalm 71; Judges 13.2–7, 24–end;
Luke 1.5–25

Monday 24 June — W
Birth of John the Baptist

Principal Service
Isaiah 40.1–11
Psalm 85.7–end
Acts 13.14b–26
or Galatians 3.23–end
Luke 1.57–66, 80

3rd Service
MP Psalms 50, 149
Ecclesiasticus 48.1–10
or Malachi 3.1–6
Luke 3.1–17

2nd Service
EP Psalms 80, 82
Malachi 4
Matthew 11.2–19

Tuesday 25 June — G
DEL week 12

Holy Communion
Genesis 13.2, 5–end
Psalm 15
Matthew 7.6, 12–14

Morning Prayer
Psalms 32, **36**
2 Chronicles 34.1–18
Romans 7.7–end

Evening Prayer
Psalm **33**
Joshua 21.43—22.8
Luke 12.13–21

Wednesday 26 June — G
Ember Day

Holy Communion
Genesis 15.1–12, 17–18
Psalm 105.1–9
Matthew 7.15–20

Psalm **34**
2 Chronicles 34.19–end
Romans 8.1–11

Psalm **119.33–56**
Joshua 22.9–end
Luke 12.22–31

Thursday 27 June — G
Cyril, bishop, teacher of the faith, 444

Holy Communion
Genesis 16.1–12, 15–16
Psalm 106.1–5
Matthew 7.21–end

Psalm 37*
2 Chronicles 35.1–19
Romans 8.12–17

Psalms 39, **40**
Joshua 23
Luke 12.32–40

Friday 28 June — Gw
Irenaeus, bishop, teacher of the faith, c.200 (see p.78)
Ember Day

Holy Communion
Genesis 17.1, 9–10, 15–22
Psalm 128
Matthew 8.1–4

Psalm **31**
2 Chronicles 35.20—36.10
Romans 8.18–30

Psalm **35**
Joshua 24.1–28
Luke 12.41–48
or: 1st EP of Peter and Paul, Apostles [or †Peter the Apostle alone]:
Psalms 66, 67; Ezekiel 3.4–11;
Galatians 1.13—2.8 [†Acts 9.32–end]

Saturday 29 June — R
Peter and Paul, Apostles
or
Peter the Apostle — R
Ember Day

Principal Service
Peter and Paul:
Zechariah 4.1–6a, 10b–end
or Acts 12.1–11
Psalm 125
Acts 12.1–11
or 2 Timothy 4.6–8, 17–18
Matthew 16.13–19

Peter alone:
Ezekiel 3.22–end
or Acts 12.1–11
Psalm 125
Acts 12.1–11
or 1 Peter 2.19–end
Matthew 16.13–19

3rd Service
MP Psalms 71, 113
Isaiah 49.1–6
Acts 11.1–18

2nd Service
EP Psalms 124, 138
Ezekiel 34.11–16
John 21.15–22

Trinity 2

Sunday 30 June — 2nd Sunday after Trinity — G
Proper 8

Principal Service
Continuous:
2 Kings 2.1–2, 6–14
Psalm 77.1–2, 11–end
[or 77.11–end]

Related:
1 Kings 19.15–16, 19–end
Psalm 16

Galatians 5.1, 13–25
Luke 9.51–end

3rd Service
Psalm 64
Deuteronomy 15.1–11
Acts 27.[13–32] 33–end

2nd Service
Psalms [59.1–6, 18–end] 60
Genesis 27.1–40
Mark 6.1–6

Monday 1 July — G
Henry, John, and Henry Venn, priests, evangelical divines, 1797, 1813, 1873
DEL week 13

Holy Communion
Genesis 18.16–end
Psalm 103.6–17
Matthew 8.18–22

Morning Prayer
Psalm 44
Ezra 1
Romans 9.1–18

Evening Prayer
Psalms 47, 49
Judges 2
Luke 13.1–9

Tuesday 2 July — G

Genesis 19.15–29
Psalm 26
Matthew 8.23–27

Psalms 48, 52
Ezra 3
Romans 9.19–end

Psalm 50
Judges 4.1–23
Luke 13.10–21
or: 1st EP of Thomas the Apostle:
Psalm 27; Isaiah 35;
Hebrews 10.35—11.1

Wednesday 3 July — R
Thomas the Apostle

Principal Service
Habakkuk 2.1–4
Psalm 31.1–6
Ephesians 2.19–end
John 20.24–29

3rd Service
MP Psalms 92, 146
2 Samuel 15.17–21
or Ecclesiasticus 2
John 11.1–16

2nd Service
EP Psalm 139
Job 42.1–6
1 Peter 1.3–12

Thursday 4 July — G

Holy Communion
Genesis 22.1–19
Psalm 116.1–7
Matthew 9.1–8

Morning Prayer
Psalms 56, **57** (63*)
Ezra 4.7–end
Romans 10.11–end

Evening Prayer
Psalms 61, **62**, 64
Judges 6.1–24
Luke 14.1–11

Friday 5 July — G

Genesis 23.1–4, 19, 24.1–8, 62–end
Psalm 106.1–5
Matthew 9.9–13

Psalms **51**, 54
Ezra 5
Romans 11.1–12

Psalm **38**
Judges 6.25–end
Luke 14.12–24

Saturday 6 July — G
Thomas More, scholar, and John Fisher, bishop, martyrs, 1535

Genesis 27.1–5a, 15–29
Psalm 135.1–6
Matthew 9.14–17

Psalm **68**
Ezra 6
Romans 11.13–24

Psalms 65, **66**
Judges 7
Luke 14.25–end

Trinity 3

		Principal Service	3rd Service	2nd Service
Sunday	**7 July** G **3rd Sunday after Trinity** Proper 9	*Continuous:* 2 Kings 5.1–14 Psalm 30 Galatians 6.[1–6]7–16 Luke 10.1–11, 16–20	*Related:* Isaiah 66.10–14 Psalm 66.1–8	Psalm 74 Deuteronomy 24.10–end Acts 28.1–16	Psalms 65 [70] Genesis 29.1–20 Mark 6.7–29

		Holy Communion	Morning Prayer	Evening Prayer
Monday	**8 July** G DEL week 14	Genesis 28.10–end Psalm 91.1–10 Matthew 9.18–26	Psalm 71 Ezra 7 Romans 11.25–end	Psalms 72, 75 Judges 8.22–end Luke 15.1–10
Tuesday	**9 July** G	Genesis 32.22–end Psalm 17.1–8 Matthew 9.32–end	Psalm 73 Ezra 8.15–end Romans 12.1–8	Psalm 74 Judges 9.1–21 Luke 15.11–end
Wednesday	**10 July** G	Genesis 41.55–end, 42.5–7, 17–end Psalm 33.1–4, 18–end Matthew 10.1–7	Psalm 77 Ezra 9 Romans 12.9–end	Psalm 119.81–104 Judges 9.22–end Luke 16.1–18
Thursday	**11 July** Gw Benedict, abbot, c.550 (see p.80)	Genesis 44.18–21, 23–29, 45.1–5 Psalm 105.11–17 Matthew 10.7–15	Psalm 78.1–39* Ezra 10.1–17 Romans 13.1–7	Psalm 78.40–end* Judges 11.1–11 Luke 16.19–end
Friday	**12 July** G	Genesis 46.1–7, 28–30 Psalm 37.3–6, 27–28 Matthew 10.16–23	Psalm 55 Nehemiah 1 Romans 13.8–end	Psalm 69 Judges 11.29–end Luke 17.1–10
Saturday	**13 July** G	Genesis 49.29–end, 50.15–25 Psalm 105.1–7 Matthew 10.24–33	Psalms 76, 79 Nehemiah 2 Romans 14.1–12	Psalms 81, 84 Judges 12.1–7 Luke 17.11–19

Trinity 4

		Principal Service		3rd Service	2nd Service
Sunday	**14 July** G **4th Sunday after Trinity** Proper 10	Continuous: Amos 7.7–end Psalm 82	Related: Deuteronomy 30.9–14 Psalm 25.1–10	Psalm 76 Deuteronomy 28.1–14 Acts 28.17–end	Psalm 77 [or 77.1–12] Genesis 32.9–30 Mark 7.1–23
		Colossians 1.1–14 Luke 10.25–37			
		Holy Communion		**Morning Prayer**	**Evening Prayer**
Monday	**15 July** Gw Swithun, bishop, c.862 (see p.79) Bonaventure, friar, bishop, teacher of the faith, 1274 DEL week 15	Exodus 1.8–14, 22 Psalm 124 Matthew 10.34—11.1		Psalms **80**, 82 Nehemiah 4 Romans 14.13–end	Psalms **85**, 86 Judges 13.1–24 Luke 17.20–end
Tuesday	**16 July** G Osmund, bishop, 1099	Exodus 2.1–15 Psalm 69.1–2, 31–end Matthew 11.20–24		Psalms 87, **89.1–18** Nehemiah 5 Romans 15.1–13	Psalm **89.19–end** Judges 14 Luke 18.1–14
Wednesday	**17 July** G	Exodus 3.1–6, 9–12 Psalm 103.1–7 Matthew 11.25–27		Psalm **119.105–128** Nehemiah 6.1—7.4 Romans 15.14–21	Psalms **91**, 93 Judges 15.1—16.3 Luke 18.15–30
Thursday	**18 July** G Elizabeth Ferard, deaconess, founder of the Community of St Andrew, 1883	Exodus 3.13–20 Psalm 105.1, 5, 8–9, 24–27 Matthew 11.28–end		Psalms 90, **92** Nehemiah 7.73b—end of 8 Romans 15.22–end	Psalm **94** Judges 16.4–end Luke 18.31–end
Friday	**19 July** Gw Gregory, bishop, and his sister Macrina, deaconess, teachers of the faith, c.394 and c.379 (see p.78)	Exodus 11.10—12.14 Psalm 116.10–end Matthew 12.1–8		Psalms **88** (95) Nehemiah 9.1–23 Romans 16.1–16	Psalm **102** Judges 17 Luke 19.1–10
Saturday	**20 July** G Margaret of Antioch, martyr, 4th cent. Bartolomé de las Casas, Apostle to the Indies, 1566	Exodus 12.37–42 Psalm 136.1–4, 10–15 Matthew 12.14–21		Psalms 96, **97**, 100 Nehemiah 9.24–end Romans 16.17–end	Psalm **104** Judges 18.1–20, 27–end Luke 19.11–27

Trinity 5

Sunday 21 July
5th Sunday after Trinity
Proper 11 *G*

Principal Service
Continuous:
Amos 8.1–12
Psalm 52

Related:
Genesis 18.1–10a
Psalm 15

Colossians 1.15–28
Luke 10.38–end

3rd Service
Psalms 82, 100
Deuteronomy 30.1–10
1 Peter 3.8–18

2nd Service
Psalm 81
Genesis 41.1–16, 25–37
1 Corinthians 4.8–13
HC John 4.31–35
or: 1st EP of Mary Magdalene:
Psalm 139; Isaiah 25.1–9;
2 Corinthians 1.3–7

Monday 22 July
Mary Magdalene *W*

Principal Service
Song of Solomon 3.1–4
Psalm 42.1–10
2 Corinthians 5.14–17
John 20.1–2, 11–18

3rd Service
MP Psalms 30, 32, 150
1 Samuel 16.14–end
Luke 8.1–3

2nd Service
EP Psalm 63
Zephaniah 3.14–end
Mark 15.40—16.7

Tuesday 23 July
Bridget, abbess, 1373 *G*
DEL week 16

Holy Communion
Exodus 14.21—15.1
Psalm 105.37–44 or *Canticle:* Exodus 15.8–10, 12, 17
Matthew 12.46–end

Morning Prayer
Psalm 106* (or 103)
Nehemiah 13.1–14
2 Corinthians 1.15—2.4

Evening Prayer
Psalm 107*
1 Samuel 1.21—2.11
Luke 19.41–end

Wednesday 24 July *G*

Holy Communion
Exodus 16.1–5, 9–15
Psalm 78.17–31
Matthew 13.1–9

Morning Prayer
Psalms 110, **111**, 112
Nehemiah 13.15–end
2 Corinthians 2.5–end

Evening Prayer
Psalm **119.129–152**
1 Samuel 2.12–26
Luke 20.1–8
or: 1st EP of James the Apostle:
Psalm 144; Deuteronomy 30.11–end;
Mark 5.21–end

Thursday 25 July
James the Apostle *R*

Principal Service
Jeremiah 45.1–5 or Acts 11.27—12.2
Psalm 126
Acts 11.27—12.2 or 2 Corinthians 4.7–15
Matthew 20.20–28

3rd Service
MP Psalms 7, 29, 117
2 Kings 1.9–15
Luke 9.46–56

2nd Service
EP Psalm 94
Jeremiah 26.1–15
Mark 1.14–20

Friday 26 July
Anne and Joachim, parents of the Blessed Virgin Mary *Gw*

Holy Communion
Exodus 20.1–17
Psalm 19.7–11
Matthew 13.18–23
Lesser Festival eucharistic lectionary:
Zephaniah 3.14–18a; Psalm 127
Romans 8.28–30; Matthew 13.16–17

Morning Prayer
Psalm **139**
Esther 2
2 Corinthians 4

Evening Prayer
Psalms **130**, 131, 137
1 Samuel 3.1—4.1a
Luke 20.20–26

Saturday 27 July
Brooke Foss Westcott, bishop, teacher of the faith, 1901 *G*

Principal Service
Exodus 24.3–8
Psalm 50.1–6, 14–15
Matthew 13.24–30

3rd Service
Psalms 120, **121**, 122
Esther 3
2 Corinthians 5

2nd Service
Psalm 118
1 Samuel 4.1b–end
Luke 20.27–40

Trinity 6

		Principal Service		3rd Service	2nd Service
Sunday	**28 July** **6th Sunday after Trinity** Proper 12	G	*Continuous:* Hosea 1.2–10 Psalm 85 [or 85.1–7] Colossians 2.6–15 [16–19] Luke 11.1–13	*Related:* Genesis 18.20–32 Psalm 138	Psalm 95 Song of Solomon 2 or 1 Maccabees 2. [1–14] 15–22 1 Peter 4.7–14	Psalm 88 [or 88.1–10] Genesis 42.1–25 1 Corinthians 10.1–24 HC Matthew 13.24–30 [31–43]

		Holy Communion		Morning Prayer	Evening Prayer
Monday	**29 July** Mary, Martha and Lazarus, companions of Our Lord DEL week 17	Gw	Exodus 32.15–24, 30–34 Psalm 106.19–23 Matthew 13.31–35 *Lesser Festival eucharistic lectionary:* Isaiah 25.6–9 Psalm 49.5–10, 16 Hebrews 2.10–15 John 12.1–8		Psalms 123, 124, 125, **126** Esther 4 2 Corinthians 6.1—7.1	Psalms **127**, 128, 129 1 Samuel 5 Luke 20.41–21.4
Tuesday	**30 July** William Wilberforce, social reformer, Olaudah Equiano and Thomas Clarkson anti-slavery campaigners, 1833, 1797 and 1846 (see p.81)	Gw	Exodus 33.7–11, 34.5–9, 28 Psalm 103.8–12 Matthew 13.36–43		Psalms **132**, 133 Esther 5 2 Corinthians 7.2–end	Psalms (134,) **135** 1 Samuel 6.1–16 Luke 21.5–19
Wednesday	**31 July** *Ignatius of Loyola, founder of the* *Society of Jesus, 1556*	G	Exodus 34.29–end Psalm 99 Matthew 13.44–46		Psalm **119.153–end** Esther 6.1–13 2 Corinthians 8.1–15	Psalm **136** 1 Samuel 7 Luke 21.20–28
Thursday	**1 August**	G	Exodus 40.16–21, 34–end Psalm 84.1–6 Matthew 13.47–53		Psalms **143**, 146 Esther 6.14—end of 7 2 Corinthians 8.16—9.5	Psalms **138**, 140, 141 1 Samuel 8 Luke 21.29–end
Friday	**2 August**	G	Leviticus 23.1, 4–11, 15–16, 27, 34–37 Psalm 81.1–8 Matthew 13.54–end		Psalms 142, **144** Esther 8 2 Corinthians 9.6–end	Psalm **145** 1 Samuel 9.1–14 Luke 22.1–13
Saturday	**3 August**	G	Leviticus 25.1, 8–17 Psalm 67 Matthew 14.1–12		Psalm **147** Esther 9.20–28 2 Corinthians 10	Psalms **148**, 149, 150 1 Samuel 9.15—10.1 Luke 22.14–23

Trinity 7

		Principal Service		3rd Service	2nd Service
Sunday	**4 August** G **7th Sunday after Trinity** Proper 13	*Continuous:* Hosea 11.1–11 Psalm 107.1–9, 43 [or 107.1–9]	*Related:* Ecclesiastes 1.2, 12–14; 2.18–23 Psalm 49.1–12 [or 49.1–9] Colossians 3.1–11 Luke 12.13–21	Psalm 106.1–10 Song of Solomon 5.2–end or 1 Maccabees 3.1–12 2 Peter 1.1–15	Psalm 107.1–32 [or 107.1–12] Genesis 50.4–end 1 Corinthians 14.1–19 HC Mark 6.45–52
		Holy Communion		**Morning Prayer**	**Evening Prayer**
Monday	**5 August** Gr Oswald, king, martyr, 642 (see p.77) DEL week 18	Numbers 11.4–15 Psalm 81.11–end Matthew 14.13–21 or 14.22–end		Psalms 1, 2, 3 Jeremiah 26 2 Corinthians 11.1–15	Psalms 4, 7 1 Samuel 10.1–16 Luke 22.24–30
		Principal Service		**3rd Service**	**2nd Service**
Tuesday	**6 August** Gold or W Transfiguration of Our Lord	Daniel 7.9–10, 13–14 Psalm 97 2 Peter 1.16–19 Luke 9.28–36		MP Psalms 27, 150 Ecclesiasticus 48.1–10 or 1 Kings 19.1–16 1 John 3.1–3	EP Psalm 72 Exodus 34.29–end 2 Corinthians 3 or: 1st EP of the Transfiguration of Our Lord: Psalms 99, 110; Exodus 24.12–end; John 12.27–36a
		Holy Communion		**Morning Prayer**	**Evening Prayer**
Wednesday	**7 August** G John Mason Neale, priest, hymn writer, 1866	Numbers 13.1–2, 25—14.1, 26–35 Psalm 106.14–24 Matthew 15.21–28		Psalm 119.1–32 Jeremiah 29.1–14 2 Corinthians 12	Psalms 11, 12, 13 1 Samuel 11 Luke 22.39–46
Thursday	**8 August** Gw Dominic, priest, founder of the Order of Preachers, 1221 (see p.80)	Numbers 20.1–13 Psalm 95.1, 8–end Matthew 16.13–23		Psalms 14, **15**, 16 Jeremiah 30.1–11 2 Corinthians 13	Psalm **18*** 1 Samuel 12 Luke 22.47–62
Friday	**9 August** Gw Mary Sumner, founder of the Mothers' Union, 1921 (see p.81)	Deuteronomy 4.32–40 Psalm 77.11–end Matthew 16.24–end		Psalms 17, **19** Jeremiah 30.12–22 James 1.1–11	Psalm **22** 1 Samuel 13.5–18 Luke 22.63–end
Saturday	**10 August** Gr Laurence, deacon, martyr, 258 (see p.77)	Deuteronomy 6.4–13 Psalm 18.1–2, 48–end Matthew 17.14–20		Psalms 20, 21, **23** Jeremiah 31.1–22 James 1.12–end	Psalms **24**, 25 1 Samuel 13.19—14.15 Luke 23.1–12

Trinity 8

		Principal Service		3rd Service	2nd Service
Sunday	**11 August** G **8th Sunday after Trinity** Proper 14	*Continuous:* Isaiah 1.1, 10–20 Psalm 50.1–8, 23–end [or 50.1–7]	*Related:* Genesis 15.1–6 Psalm 33.12–end [or 33.12–21] Hebrews 11.1–3, 8–16 Luke 12.32–40	Psalm 115 Song of Solomon 8.5–7 or 1 Maccabees 14.4–15 2 Peter 3.8–13	Psalms 108 [116] Isaiah 11.10—end of 12 2 Corinthians 1.1–22 HC Mark 7.24–30
		Holy Communion		**Morning Prayer**	**Evening Prayer**
Monday	**12 August** G DEL week 19	Deuteronomy 10.12–end Psalm 147.13–end Matthew 17.22–end		Psalms 27, **30** Jeremiah 31.23–25, 27–37 James 2.1–13	Psalms 26, **28**, 29 1 Samuel 14.24–46 Luke 23.13–25
Tuesday	**13 August** Gw Jeremy Taylor, bishop, teacher of the faith, 1667 (see p.78) Florence Nightingale, nurse, social reformer, 1910 Octavia Hill, social reformer, 1912	Deuteronomy 31.1–8 Psalm 107.1–3, 42–end or *Canticle:* Deuteronomy 32.3–4, 7–9 Matthew 18.1–5, 10, 12–14		Psalms 32, **36** Jeremiah 32.1–15 James 2.14–end	Psalm **33** 1 Samuel 15.1–23 Luke 23.26–43
Wednesday	**14 August** G *Maximilian Kolbe, friar, martyr, 1941*	Deuteronomy 34 Psalm 66.14–end Matthew 18.15–20		Psalm **34** Jeremiah 33.1–13 James 3	Psalm 1**19.33–56** 1 Samuel 16 Luke 23.44–56a *or:* 1st EP of the Blessed Virgin Mary: Psalm 72; Proverbs 8.22–31; John 19.23–27
		Principal Service		**3rd Service**	**2nd Service**
Thursday	**15 August** W The Blessed Virgin Mary	Isaiah 61.10–end *or* Revelation 11.19—12.6, 10 Psalm 45.10–end Galatians 4.4–7 Luke 1.46–55		MP Psalms 98, 138, 147.1–12 Isaiah 7.10–15 Luke 11.27–28	EP Psalm 132 Song of Solomon 2.1–7 Acts 1.6–14
		Holy Communion		**Morning Prayer**	**Evening Prayer**
Friday	**16 August** G	Joshua 24.1–13 Psalm 136.1–3, 16–22 Matthew 19.3–12		Psalm **31** Jeremiah 35 James 4.13—5.6	Psalm **35** 1 Samuel 17.31–54 Luke 24.13–35
Saturday	**17 August** G	Joshua 24.14–29 Psalm 16.1, 5–end Matthew 19.13–15		Psalms 41, **42**, 43 Jeremiah 36.1–18 James 5.7–end	Psalms 45, **46** 1 Samuel 17.55—18.16 Luke 24.36–end

Trinity 9

Sunday 18 August — 9th Sunday after Trinity — G
Proper 15

Principal Service
Continuous:
Isaiah 5.1–7
Psalm 80.1–2, 9–end
[or 80.9–end]

Related:
Jeremiah 23.23–29
Psalm 82

Hebrews 11.29—12.2
Luke 12.49–56

3rd Service
Psalm 119.33–48
Jonah 1
or Ecclesiasticus 3.1–15
2 Peter 3.14–end

2nd Service
Psalm 119.17–32 [or 119.17–24]
Isaiah 28.9–22
2 Corinthians 8.1–9
HC Matthew 20.1–16

Monday 19 August — G
DEL week 20

Holy Communion
Judges 2.11–19
Psalm 106.34–42
Matthew 19.16–22

Morning Prayer
Psalm 44
Jeremiah 36.19–end
Mark 1.1–13

Evening Prayer
Psalms 47, 49
1 Samuel 19.1–18
Acts 1.1–14

Tuesday 20 August — Gw
Bernard, abbot, teacher of the faith, 1153 (see p.78)
William and Catherine Booth, founders of the Salvation Army, 1912, 1890

Judges 6.11–24
Psalm 85.8–end
Matthew 19.23–end

Psalms 48, 52
Jeremiah 37
Mark 1.14–20

Psalm 50
1 Samuel 20.1–17
Acts 1.15–end

Wednesday 21 August — G

Judges 9.6–15
Psalm 21.1–6
Matthew 20.1–16

Psalm 119.57–80
Jeremiah 38.1–13
Mark 1.21–28

Psalms 59, 60 (67)
1 Samuel 20.18–end
Acts 2.1–21

Thursday 22 August — G

Judges 11.29–end
Psalm 40.4–11
Matthew 22.1–14

Psalms 56, 57 (63*)
Jeremiah 38.14–end
Mark 1.29–end

Psalms 61, 62, 64
1 Samuel 21.1—22.5
Acts 2.22–36

Friday 23 August — G

Ruth 1.1, 3–6, 14–16, 22
Psalm 146
Matthew 22.34–40

Psalms 51, 54
Jeremiah 39
Mark 2.1–12

Psalm 38
1 Samuel 22.6–end
Acts 2.37–end
or: 1st EP of Bartholomew the Apostle:
Psalm 97; Isaiah 61.1–9;
2 Corinthians 6.1–10

Saturday 24 August — Bartholomew the Apostle — R

Principal Service
Isaiah 43.8–13 or Acts 5.12–16
Psalm 145.1–7
Acts 5.12–16 or 1 Corinthians 4.9–15
Luke 22.24–30

3rd Service
MP Psalms 86, 117
Genesis 28.10–17
John 1.43–end

2nd Service
EP Psalms 91, 116
Ecclesiasticus 39.1–10
or Deuteronomy 18.15–19
Matthew 10.1–22

Trinity 10

Sunday

25 August — G
10th Sunday after Trinity
Proper 16

Principal Service
Continuous:
Jeremiah 1.4–10
Psalm 71.1–6

Related:
Isaiah 58.9b–end
Psalm 103.1–8

Hebrews 12.18–end
Luke 13.10–17

3rd Service
Psalm 119.73–88
Jonah 2
or Ecclesiasticus 3.17–29
Revelation 1

2nd Service
Psalm 119.49–72 [or 119.49–56]
Isaiah 30.8–21
2 Corinthians 9
HC Matthew 21.28–32

Monday

26 August — G
DEL week 21

Holy Communion
1 Thessalonians 1.1–5, 8–end
Psalm 149.1–5
Matthew 23.13–22

Morning Prayer
Psalm 71
Jeremiah 41
Mark 2.23—3.6

Evening Prayer
Psalms 72, 75
1 Samuel 24
Acts 3.11–end

Tuesday

27 August — Gw
Monica, mother of Augustine of Hippo, 387 (see p.81)

1 Thessalonians 2.1–8
Psalm 139.1–9
Matthew 23.23–26

Psalm 73
Jeremiah 42
Mark 3.7–19a

Psalm 74
1 Samuel 26
Acts 4.1–12

Wednesday

28 August — Gw
Augustine, bishop, teacher of the faith, 430 (see p.78)

1 Thessalonians 2.9–13
Psalm 126
Matthew 23.27–32

Psalm 77
Jeremiah 43
Mark 3.19b–end

Psalm 119.81–104
1 Samuel 28.3–end
Acts 4.13–31

Thursday

29 August — Gr
Beheading of John the Baptist

1 Thessalonians 3.7–end
Psalm 90.13–end
Matthew 24.42–end
Lesser Festival eucharistic lectionary:
Jeremiah 1.4–10
Psalm 11
Hebrews 11.32—12.2
Matthew 14.1–12

Psalm 78.1–39*
Jeremiah 44.1–14
Mark 4.1–20

Psalm 78.40–end*
1 Samuel 31
Acts 4.32—5.11

Friday

30 August — Gw
John Bunyan, spiritual writer, 1688 (see p.78)

1 Thessalonians 4.1–8
Psalm 97
Matthew 25.1–13

Psalm 55
Jeremiah 44.15–end
Mark 4.21–34

Psalm 69
2 Samuel 1
Acts 5.12–26

Saturday

31 August — Gw
Aidan, bishop, missionary, 651 (see p.80)

1 Thessalonians 4.9–12
Psalm 98.1–2, 8–end
Matthew 25.14–30

Psalms 76, 79
Jeremiah 45
Mark 4.35–end

Psalms 81, 84
2 Samuel 2.1–11
Acts 5.27–end

Trinity 11

		Principal Service		3rd Service	2nd Service
Sunday	1 September G 11th Sunday after Trinity Proper 17	Continuous: Jeremiah 2.4–13 Psalm 81.1, 10–end [or 81.1–11]	Related: Ecclesiasticus 10.12–18 or Proverbs 25.6–7 Psalm 112 Hebrews 13.1–8, 15–16 Luke 14.1, 7–14	Psalm 119.161–end Jonah 3.1–9 or Ecclesiasticus 11. [7–17] 18–28 Revelation 3.14–22	Psalm 119.81–96 [or 119.81–88] Isaiah 33.13–22 John 3.22–36
		Holy Communion		Morning Prayer	Evening Prayer
Monday	2 September G *Martyrs of Papua New Guinea, 1901, 1942* DEL week 22	1 Thessalonians 4.13–end Psalm 96 Luke 4.16–30		Psalms 80, 82 Micah 1.1–9 Mark 5.1–20	Psalms 85, 86 2 Samuel 3.12–end Acts 6
Tuesday	3 September Gw *Gregory the Great, bishop, teacher of the faith, 604 (see p.78)*	1 Thessalonians 5.1–6, 9–11 Psalm 27.1–8 Luke 4.31–37		Psalms 87, **89.1–18** Micah 2 Mark 5.21–34	Psalm **89.19–end** 2 Samuel 5.1–12 Acts 7.1–16
Wednesday	4 September G *Birinus, bishop, 650*	Colossians 1.1–8 Psalm 34.11–18 Luke 4.38–end		Psalm 119.105–128 Micah 3 Mark 5.35–end	Psalms **91**, 93 2 Samuel 6.1–19 Acts 7.17–43
Thursday	5 September G	Colossians 1.9–14 Psalm 98.1–5 Luke 5.1–11		Psalms 90, **92** Micah 4.1—5.1 Mark 6.1–13	Psalm **94** 2 Samuel 7.1–17 Acts 7.44–53
Friday	6 September G *Allen Gardiner, missionary, founder of the South American Mission Society, 1851*	Colossians 1.15–20 Psalm 89.19b–28 Luke 5.33–end		Psalms **88** (95) Micah 5.2–end Mark 6.14–29	Psalm **102** 2 Samuel 7.18–end Acts 7.54—8.3
Saturday	7 September G	Colossians 1.21–23 Psalm 117 Luke 6.1–5		Psalms 96, **97**, 100 Micah 6 Mark 6.30–44	Psalm **104** 2 Samuel 9 Acts 8.4–25

Trinity 12

		Principal Service		3rd Service	2nd Service
Sunday	**8 September** **12th Sunday after Trinity** Proper 18 G	Continuous: Jeremiah 18.1–11 Psalm 139.1–5, 12–18 [or 139.1–7] Philemon 1–21 Luke 14.25–33	Related: Deuteronomy 30.15–end Psalm 1	Psalms 122, 123 Jonah 3.10—end of 4 or Ecclesiasticus 27.30—28.9 Revelation 8.1–5	Psalms [120] 121 Isaiah 43.14—44.5 John 5.30–end

		Holy Communion	Morning Prayer	Evening Prayer
Monday	**9 September** G *Charles Fuge Lowder, priest, 1880* DEL week 23	Colossians 1.24—2.3 Psalm 62.1–7 Luke 6.6–11	Psalms **98**, 99, 101 Micah 7.1–7 Mark 6.45–end	Psalm **105*** (or 103) 2 Samuel 11 Acts 8.26–end
Tuesday	**10 September** G	Colossians 2.6–15 Psalm 8 Luke 6.12–19	Psalm **106*** (or 103) Micah 7.8–end Mark 7.1–13	Psalm **107*** 2 Samuel 12.1–25 Acts 9.1–19a
Wednesday	**11 September** G	Colossians 3.1–11 Psalm 15 Luke 6.20–26	Psalms 110, **111**, 112 Habakkuk 1.1–11 Mark 7.14–23	Psalm **119.129–152** 2 Samuel 15.1–12 Acts 9.19b–31
Thursday	**12 September** G	Colossians 3.12–17 Psalm 149.1–5 Luke 6.27–38	Psalms 113, **115** Habakkuk 1.12—2.5 Mark 7.24–30	Psalms 114, **116**, 117 2 Samuel 15.13–end Acts 9.32–end
Friday	**13 September** Gw *John Chrysostom, bishop,* *teacher of the faith, 407 (see p.78)*	1 Timothy 1.1–2, 12–14 Psalm 16 Luke 6.39–42	Psalm **139** Habakkuk 2.6–end Mark 7.31–end	Psalms **130**, 131, 137 2 Samuel 16.1–14 Acts 10.1–16 or: 1st EP of Holy Cross Day: Psalm 66; Isaiah 52.13—end of 53; Ephesians 2.11–end

		Principal Service	3rd Service	2nd Service
Saturday	**14 September** R Holy Cross Day	Numbers 21.4–9 Psalm 22.23–28 Philippians 2.6–11 John 3.13–17	MP Psalms 2, 8, 146 Genesis 3.1–15 John 12.27–36a	EP Psalms 110, 150 Isaiah 63.1–16 1 Corinthians 1.18–25

Trinity 13

		Principal Service		3rd Service	2nd Service
Sunday	**15 September** G **13th Sunday after Trinity** Proper 19	Continuous: Jeremiah 4.11–12, 22–28 Psalm 14 1 Timothy 1.12–17 Luke 15.1–10	Related: Exodus 32.7–14 Psalm 51.1–11	Psalms 126, 127 Isaiah 44.24—45.8 Revelation 12.1–12	Psalms 124, 125 Isaiah 60 John 6.51–69
		Holy Communion		**Morning Prayer**	**Evening Prayer**
Monday	**16 September** Gw Ninian, bishop, apostle of the Picts, c.432 (see p.80) Edward Bouverie Pusey, priest, 1882 DEL week 24	1 Timothy 2.1–8 Psalm 28 Luke 7.1–10		Psalms 123, 124, 125, **126** Haggai 1.1–11 Mark 8.11–21	Psalms **127**, 128, 129 2 Samuel 18.1–18 Acts 10.34–end
Tuesday	**17 September** Gw Hildegard, abbess, visionary, 1179 (see p.80)	1 Timothy 3.1–13 Psalm 101 Luke 7.11–17		Psalms **132**, 133 Haggai 1.12—2.9 Mark 8.22–26	Psalms (134,) **135** 2 Samuel 18.19—19.8a Acts 11.1–18
Wednesday	**18 September** G	1 Timothy 3.14–end Psalm 111.1–5 Luke 7.31–35		Psalm **119.153–end** Haggai 2.10–end Mark 8.27—9.1	Psalm **136** 2 Samuel 19.8b–23 Acts 11.19–end
Thursday	**19 September** G Theodore, archbishop, 690	1 Timothy 4.12–end Psalm 111.6–end Luke 7.36–end		Psalms **143**, 146 Zechariah 1.1–17 Mark 9.2–13	Psalms **138**, 140, 141 2 Samuel 19.24–end Acts 12.1–17
Friday	**20 September** Gr John Coleridge Patteson, bishop, and companions, martyrs, 1871 (see p.77)	1 Timothy 6.2b–12 Psalm 49.1–9 Luke 8.1–3		Psalms 142, **144** Zechariah 1.18—end of 2 Mark 9.14–29	Psalm **145** 2 Samuel 23.1–7 Acts 12.18–end or: 1st EP of Matthew, Apostle and Evangelist: Psalm 34; Isaiah 33.13–17; Matthew 6.19–end
		Principal Service		**3rd Service**	**2nd Service**
Saturday	**21 September** R Matthew, Apostle and Evangelist	Proverbs 3.13–18 Psalm 119.65–72 2 Corinthians 4.1–6 Matthew 9.9–13		MP Psalms 49, 117 1 Kings 19.15–end 2 Timothy 3.14–end	EP Psalm 119.33–40, 89–96 Ecclesiastes 5.4–12 Matthew 19.16–end

53

Trinity 14

		Principal Service	3rd Service	2nd Service
Sunday	**22 September** G **14th Sunday after Trinity** Proper 20	*Continuous:* Jeremiah 8.18—9.1 Psalm 79.1–9 1 Timothy 2.1–7 Luke 16.1–13	Psalms 130, 131 Isaiah 45.9–22 Revelation 14.1–5	Psalms [128] 129 Ezra 1 John 7.14–36
		Related: Amos 8.4–7 Psalm 113		
		Holy Communion	**Morning Prayer**	**Evening Prayer**
Monday	**23 September** G DEL week 25	Ezra 1.1–6 Psalm 126 Luke 8.16–18	Psalms 1, 2, 3 Zechariah 4 Mark 9.38–end	Psalms 4, 7 1 Kings 1.5–31 Acts 13.13–43
Tuesday	**24 September** G	Ezra 6.7–8, 12, 14–20 Psalm 124 Luke 8.19–21	Psalms 5, 6 (8) Zechariah 6.9–end Mark 10.1–16	Psalms 9, 10* 1 Kings 1.32—2.4; 2.10–12 Acts 13.44—14.7
Wednesday	**25 September** Gw Lancelot Andrewes, bishop, spiritual writer, 1626 (see p.79) Sergei of Radonezh, monastic reformer, teacher of the faith, 1392 Ember Day	Ezra 9.5–9 *Canticle:* Song of Tobit or Psalm 103.1–6 Luke 9.1–6	Psalm 119.1–32 Zechariah 7 Mark 10.17–31	Psalms 11, 12, 13 1 Kings 3 Acts 14.8–end
Thursday	**26 September** G *Wilson Carlile, founder of the Church Army,* *1942*	Haggai 1.1–8 Psalm 149.1–5 Luke 9.7–9	Psalms 14, 15, 16 Zechariah 8.1–8 Mark 10.32–34	Psalm 18* 1 Kings 4.29—5.12 Acts 15.1–21
Friday	**27 September** Gw Vincent de Paul, founder of the Lazarists, 1660 (see p.80) Ember Day	Haggai 1.15b—2.9 Psalm 43 Luke 9.18–22	Psalms 17, 19 Zechariah 8.9–end Mark 10.35–45	Psalm 22 1 Kings 6.1, 11–28 Acts 15.22–35
Saturday	**28 September** G Ember Day	Zechariah 2.1–5, 10–11 Psalm 125 or *Canticle:* Jeremiah 31.10–13 Luke 9.43b–45	Psalms 20, 21, 23 Zechariah 9.1–12 Mark 10.46–end	Psalms 24, 25 1 Kings 8.1–30 Acts 15.36—16.5 or: 1st EP of Michael and All Angels: Psalm 91; 2 Kings 6.8–17; Matthew 18.1–6, 10

Michael and All Angels / Trinity 15

If Michael and All Angels is celebrated on Sunday 29 September:

		Principal Service	**3rd Service**	**2nd Service**
Sunday	**29 September** W Michael and All Angels	Genesis 28.10–17 or Revelation 12.7–12 Psalm 103.19–end Revelation 12.7–12 or Hebrews 1.5–end John 1.47–end	*MP* Psalms 34, 150 Tobit 12.6–end or Daniel 12.1–4 Acts 12.1–11	*EP* Psalms 138, 148 Daniel 10.4–end Revelation 5
		Holy Communion	**Morning Prayer**	**Evening Prayer**
Monday	**30 September** G *Jerome, translator, teacher of the faith, 420* DEL week 26	Zechariah 8.1–8 Psalm 102.12–22 Luke 9.46–50	Psalms 27, **30** Zechariah 10 Mark 11.1–11	Psalms 26, **28**, 29 1 Kings 8.31–62 Acts 16.6–24

If Michael and All Angels is transferred to Monday 30 September:

		Principal Service		**3rd Service**	**2nd Service**
Sunday	**29 September** G **15th Sunday after Trinity** Proper 21	*Continuous:* Jeremiah 32.1–3a, 6–15 Psalm 91.1–6, 14–end [or 91.11–end] 1 Timothy 6.6–19 Luke 16.19–end	*Related:* Amos 6.1a, 4–7 Psalm 146	Psalm 132 Isaiah 48.12–end Luke 11.37–end	Psalms 134, 135 [or 135.1–14] Nehemiah 2 John 8.31–38, 48–end *or:* 1st EP of Michael and All Angels: Psalm 91; 2 Kings 6.8–17; Matthew 18.1–6, 10
Monday	**30 September** W Michael and All Angels *(transferred from 29 September)*	Genesis 28.10–17 or Revelation 12.7–12 Psalm 103.19–end Revelation 12.7–12 or Hebrews 1.5–end John 1.47–end		*MP* Psalms 34, 150 Tobit 12.6–end or Daniel 12.1–4 Acts 12.1–11	*EP* Psalms 138, 148 Daniel 10.4–end Revelation 5

Trinity 15

			Holy Communion	Morning Prayer	Evening Prayer
Tuesday	1 October *Remigius, bishop, 533* *Anthony Ashley Cooper (Earl of Shaftesbury),* *social reformer, 1885* DEL week 26	G	Zechariah 8.20–end Psalm 87 Luke 9.51–56	Psalms 32, **36** Zechariah 11.4–end Mark 11.12–26	Psalm **33** 1 Kings 8.63—9.9 Acts 16.25–end
Wednesday	2 October	G	Nehemiah 2.1–8 Psalm 137.1–6 Luke 9.57–end	Psalm **34** Zechariah 12.1–10 Mark 11.27–end	Psalm 1**19.33–56** 1 Kings 10.1–25 Acts 17.1–15
Thursday	3 October *George Bell, bishop, ecumenist,* *peacemaker, 1958*	G	Nehemiah 8.1–12 Psalm 19.7–11 Luke 10.1–12	Psalm **37*** Zechariah 13 Mark 12.1–12	Psalms 39, **40** 1 Kings 11.1–13 Acts 17.16–end
Friday	4 October *Francis of Assisi, friar, deacon, 1226* (see p.80)	Gw	Baruch 1.15–end or Deuteronomy 31.7–13 Psalm 79.1–9 Luke 10.13–16	Psalm **31** Zechariah 14.1–11 Mark 12.13–17	Psalm **35** 1 Kings 11.26–end Acts 18.1–21
Saturday	5 October	G	Baruch 4.5–12, 27–29 or Joshua 22.1–6 Psalm 69.33–37 Luke 10.17–24	Psalms 41, **42**, 43 Zechariah 14.12–end Mark 12.18–27	Psalms 45, **46** 1 Kings 12.1–24 Acts 18.22—19.7

Trinity 16

		Principal Service		3rd Service	2nd Service
Sunday	**6 October** 16th Sunday after Trinity Proper 22	G	Continuous: Lamentations 1.1–6 Canticle: Lamentations 3.19–26 or Psalm 137 [or 137.1–6] 2 Timothy 1.1–14 Luke 17.5–10	Related: Habakkuk 1.1–4; 2.1–4 Psalm 37.1–9	Psalm 141 Isaiah 49.13–23 Luke 12.1–12	Psalm 142 Nehemiah 5.1–13 John 9

		Holy Communion	Morning Prayer	Evening Prayer
Monday	**7 October** DEL week 27	G	Jonah 1.1—2.2, 10 Canticle: Jonah 2.2–4, 7 or Psalm 69.1–6 Luke 10.25–37	Psalm **44** Ecclesiasticus 1.1–10 or Ezekiel 1.1–14 Mark 12.28–34	Psalms **47**, 49 1 Kings 12.25—13.10 Acts 19.8–20
Tuesday	**8 October**	G	Jonah 3 Psalm 130 Luke 10.38–end	Psalms **48**, 52 Ecclesiasticus 1.11–end or Ezekiel 1.15—2.2 Mark 12.35–end	Psalm **50** 1 Kings 13.11–end Acts 19.21–end
Wednesday	**9 October** Denys, bishop, and companions, martyrs, c.250 Robert Grosseteste, bishop, philosopher, scientist, 1253	G	Jonah 4 Psalm 86.1–9 Luke 11.1–4	Psalm 1**19.57–80** Ecclesiasticus 2 or Ezekiel 2.3—3.11 Mark 13.1–13	Psalms **59**, 60 (67) 1 Kings 17 Acts 20.1–16
Thursday	**10 October** Paulinus, bishop, missionary, 644 (see p.80) Thomas Traherne, poet, spiritual writer, 1674	Gw	Malachi 3.13—4.2a Psalm 1 Luke 11.5–13	Psalms 56, **57** (63*) Ecclesiasticus 3.17–29 or Ezekiel 3.12–end Mark 13.14–23	Psalms 61, **62**, 64 1 Kings 18.1–20 Acts 20.17–end
Friday	**11 October** Ethelburga, abbess, 675 James the Deacon, companion of Paulinus, 7th cent.	G	Joel 1.13–15, 2.1–2 Psalm 9.1–7 Luke 11.15–26	Psalms **51**, 54 Ecclesiasticus 4.11–28 or Ezekiel 8 Mark 13.24–31	Psalm **38** 1 Kings 18.21–end Acts 21.1–16
Saturday	**12 October** Wilfrid, bishop, missionary, 709 (see p.80) Elizabeth Fry, prison reformer, 1845 Edith Cavell, nurse, 1915	Gw	Joel 3.12–end Psalm 97.1, 8–end Luke 11.27–28	Psalm **68** Ecclesiasticus 4.29—6.1 or Ezekiel 9 Mark 13.32–end	Psalms 65, **66** 1 Kings 19 Acts 21.17–36

Trinity 17

		Principal Service		3rd Service	2nd Service
Sunday	**13 October** G **17th Sunday after Trinity** Proper 23	*Continuous:* Jeremiah 29.1, 4–7 Psalm 66.1–11	*Related:* 2 Kings 5.1–3, 7–15c Psalm 111 2 Timothy 2.8–15 Luke 17.11–19	Psalm 143 Isaiah 50.4–10 Luke 13.22–30	Psalm 144 Nehemiah 6.1–16 John 15.12–end

		Holy Communion	Morning Prayer	Evening Prayer
Monday	**14 October** G DEL week 28	Romans 1.1–7 Psalm 98 Luke 11.29–32	Psalm **71** Ecclesiasticus 6.14–end or Ezekiel 10.1–19 Mark 14.1–11	Psalms **72**, 75 1 Kings 21 Acts 21.37—22.21
Tuesday	**15 October** Gw Teresa of Avila, teacher of the faith, 1582 (see p.78)	Romans 1.16–25 Psalm 19.1–4 Luke 11.37–41	Psalm **73** Ecclesiasticus 7.27–end or Ezekiel 11.14–end Mark 14.12–25	Psalm **74** 1 Kings 22.1–28 Acts 22.22—23.11
Wednesday	**16 October** G *Nicholas Ridley and Hugh Latimer, bishops, martyrs, 1555*	Romans 2.1–11 Psalm 62.1–8 Luke 11.42–46	Psalm **77** Ecclesiasticus 10.6–8, 12–24 or Ezekiel 12.1–16 Mark 14.26–42	Psalm **119.81–104** 1 Kings 22.29–45 Acts 23.12–end
Thursday	**17 October** Gr Ignatius, bishop, martyr, c.107 (see p.77)	Romans 3.21–30 Psalm 130 Luke 11.47–end	Psalm **78.1–39*** Ecclesiasticus 11.7–28 or Ezekiel 12.17–end Mark 14.43–52	Psalm **78.40–end*** 2 Kings 1.2–17 Acts 24.1–23 *or:* 1st EP of Luke the Evangelist: Psalm 33; Hosea 6.1–3; 2 Timothy 3.10–end

		Principal Service	3rd Service	2nd Service
Friday	**18 October** R **Luke the Evangelist**	Isaiah 35.3–6 or Acts 16.6–12a Psalm 147.1–7 2 Timothy 4.5–17 Luke 10.1–9	MP Psalms 145, 146 Isaiah 55 Luke 1.1–4	EP Psalm 103 Ecclesiasticus 38.1–14 or Isaiah 61.1–6 Colossians 4.7–end

		Holy Communion	Morning Prayer	Evening Prayer
Saturday	**19 October** Gw Henry Martyn, translator, missionary, 1812 (see p.80)	Romans 4.13, 16–18 Psalm 105.6–10, 41–44 Luke 12.8–12	Psalms **76**, 79 Ecclesiasticus 15.11–end or Ezekiel 14.1–11 Mark 14.66–end	Psalms 81, **84** 2 Kings 4.1–37 Acts 25.13–end

Trinity 18

		Principal Service		3rd Service	2nd Service
Sunday	**20 October** **18th Sunday after Trinity** Proper 24 G	*Continuous:* Jeremiah 31.27–34 Psalm 119.97–104	*Related:* Genesis 32.22–31 Psalm 121	Psalm 147 Isaiah 54.1–14 Luke 13.31–end	Psalms [146] 149 Nehemiah 8.9–end John 16.1–11
		2 Timothy 3.14—4.5 Luke 18.1–8			
		Holy Communion		**Morning Prayer**	**Evening Prayer**
Monday	**21 October** DEL week 29 G	Romans 4.20–end Canticle: Benedictus 1–6 Luke 12.13–21		Psalms **80**, 82 Ecclesiasticus 16.17–end or Ezekiel 14.12–end Mark 15.1–15	Psalms **85**, 86 2 Kings 5 Acts 26.1–23
Tuesday	**22 October** G	Romans 5.12, 15, 17–end Psalm 40.7–12 Luke 12.35–38		Psalms 87, **89.1–18** Ecclesiasticus 17.1–24 or Ezekiel 18.1–20 Mark 15.16–32	Psalm **89.19–end** 2 Kings 6.1–23 Acts 26.24–end
Wednesday	**23 October** G	Romans 6.12–18 Psalm 124 Luke 12.39–48		Psalm 119.**105–128** Ecclesiasticus 18.1–14 or Ezekiel 18.21–32 Mark 15.33–41	Psalms **91**, 93 2 Kings 9.1–16 Acts 27.1–26
Thursday	**24 October** G	Romans 6.19–end Psalm 1 Luke 12.49–53		Psalms 90, **92** Ecclesiasticus 19.4–17 or Ezekiel 20.1–20 Mark 15.42–end	Psalm **94** 2 Kings 9.17–end Acts 27.27–end
Friday	**25 October** G *Crispin and Crispinian, martyrs, c.287*	Romans 7.18–end Psalm 119.33–40 Luke 12.54–end		Psalms **88** (95) Ecclesiasticus 19.20–end or Ezekiel 20.21–38 Mark 16.1–8	Psalm 102 2 Kings 12.1–19 Acts 28.1–16
Saturday	**26 October** Gw *Alfred, king, scholar, 899 (see p.81)* *Cedd, abbot, bishop, 664*	Romans 8.1–11 Psalm 24.1–6 Luke 13.1–9		Psalms 96, **97**, 100 Ecclesiasticus 21.1–17 or Ezekiel 24.15–end Mark 16.9–end	Psalm 104 2 Kings 17.1–23 Acts 28.17–end

Last after Trinity

		Principal Service	3rd Service	2nd Service
Sunday	**27 October** **Last Sunday after Trinity** Proper 25 G	*Continuous:* Joel 2.23–end Psalm 65 [or 65.1–7] *Related:* Ecclesiasticus 35.12–17 or Jeremiah 14.7–10, 19–end Psalm 84.1–7 2 Timothy 4.6–8, 16–18 Luke 18.9–14	Psalm 119.105–128 Isaiah 59.9–20 Luke 14.1–14	Psalm 119.1–16 Ecclesiastes 11, 12 2 Timothy 2.1–7 HC Matthew 22.34–end *or:* 1st EP of Simon and Jude, Apostles: Psalms 124, 125, 126; Deuteronomy 32.1–4; John 14.15–26
or Sunday	**27 October** **Bible Sunday** G	Isaiah 45.22–end Psalm 119.129–136 Romans 15.1–6 Luke 4.16–24	Psalm 119.105–128 1 Kings 22.1–17 Romans 15.4–13 or Luke 14.1–14	Psalm 119.1–16 Jeremiah 36.9–end Romans 10.5–17 HC Matthew 22.34–40 *or:* 1st EP of Simon and Jude, Apostles: Psalms 124, 125, 126; Deuteronomy 32.1–4; John 14.15–26

or, if the date of dedication of a church is not known, the Dedication Festival (Gold or W) may be celebrated today or on 6 October, or on a suitable date chosen locally (see p.75)

		Holy Communion	Morning Prayer	Evening Prayer
Monday	**28 October** Simon and Jude, Apostles R	Isaiah 28.14–16 Psalm 119.89–96 Ephesians 2.19–end John 15.17–end	MP Psalms 116, 117 Wisdom 5.1–16 or Isaiah 45.18–end Luke 6.12–16	EP Psalm 119.1–16 1 Maccabees 2.42–66 or Isaiah 3.11–18 Jude 1–4, 17–end
Tuesday	**29 October** James Hannington, bishop, martyr, 1885 (see p.77) DEL week 30 Gr	Romans 8.18–25 Psalm 126 Luke 13.18–21	Psalm **106*** (or 103) Ecclesiasticus 22.27—23.15 or Ezekiel 33.1–20 John 13.12–20	Psalm **107*** 2 Kings 18.1–12 Philippians 1.12–end
Wednesday	**30 October** G	Romans 8.26–30 Psalm 13 Luke 13.22–30	Psalms 110, **111**, 112 Ecclesiasticus 24.1–22 or Ezekiel 33.21–end John 13.21–30	Psalm **119.129–152** 2 Kings 18.13–end Philippians 2.1–13
Thursday	**31 October** *Martin Luther, reformer, 1546* G	Romans 8.31–end Psalm 109.20–26, 29–30 Luke 13.31–end	Psalms 113, **115** Ecclesiasticus 24.23–end or Ezekiel 34.1–16 John 13.31–end	Psalms 114, **116**, 117 2 Kings 19.1–19 Philippians 2.14–end *Or, if All Saints' Day is celebrated on Friday 1 November only:* **1st EP of All Saints' Day:** Psalms 1, 5; Ecclesiasticus 44.1–15 or Isaiah 40.27–end; Revelation 19.6–10

All Saints' Day / 4 before Advent

All Saints' Day is celebrated either on Friday 1 November or on Sunday 3 November; if the latter there may be a supplementary celebration on 1 November. If All Saints' Day is celebrated on Friday 1 November only:

			Principal Service	3rd Service	2nd Service
Friday	1 November All Saints' Day	Gold or W	Daniel 7.1–3, 15–18 Psalm 149 Ephesians 1.11–end Luke 6.20–31	MP Psalms 15, 84, 149 Isaiah 35.1–9 Luke 9.18–27	EP Psalms 148, 150 Isaiah 65.17–end Hebrews 11.32—12.2

If All Saints' Day is celebrated on Friday 1 November in addition to Sunday 3 November:

			Principal Service	3rd Service	2nd Service
Friday	1 November All Saints' Day	Gold or W	Isaiah 56.3–8 or 2 Esdras 2.42–end Psalm 33.1–5 Hebrews 12.18–24 Matthew 5.1–12	MP Psalms 111, 112, 117 Wisdom 5.1–16 or Jeremiah 31.31–34 2 Corinthians 4.5–12	EP Psalm 145 Isaiah 66.20–23 Colossians 1.9–14
			Holy Communion	Morning Prayer	Evening Prayer
Saturday	2 November Commemoration of the Faithful Departed (All Souls' Day)	Rp/Gp	Romans 11.1–2, 11–12, 25–29 Psalm 94.14–19 Luke 14.1, 7–11 Lesser Festival eucharistic lectionary: Lamentations 3.17–26, 31–33 or Wisdom 3.1–9 Psalm 23 or 27.1–6,16–17 Romans 5.5–11 or 1 Peter 1.3–9 John 5.19–25 or John 6.37–40	Psalms 120, 121, 122 Ecclesiasticus 28.14–end or Ezekiel 36.16–36 John 14.15–end	Psalm 118 2 Kings 20 Philippians 4.2–end
			Principal Service	3rd Service	2nd Service
Sunday	3 November 4th Sunday before Advent	R/G	Isaiah 1.10–18 Psalm 32.1–8 2 Thessalonians 1 Luke 19.1–10	Psalm 87 Job 26 Colossians 1.9–14	Psalm 145 [or 145.1–9] Lamentations 3.22–33 John 11. [1–31] 32–44

61

All Saints' Day

If All Saints' Day is celebrated on Sunday 3 November only:

			Holy Communion	**Morning Prayer**	**Evening Prayer**
Friday	1 November	G	Romans 9.1–5 Psalm 147.13–end Luke 14.1–6	Psalm **139** Ecclesiasticus 27.30—28.9 *or* Ezekiel 34.17–end John 14.1–14	Psalms **130**, 131, 137 2 Kings 19.20–36 Philippians 3.1—4.1
Saturday	2 November Commemoration of the Faithful Departed (All Souls' Day)	Gp	Romans 11.1–2, 11–12, 25–29 Psalm 94.14–19 Luke 14.1, 7–11 *Lesser Festival eucharistic lectionary:* Lamentations 3.17–26, 31–33 *or* Wisdom 3.1–9 Psalm 23 *or* 27.1–6, 16–17 Romans 5.5–11 *or* 1 Peter 1.3–9 John 5.19–25 *or* John 6.37–40	Psalms **120**, 121, **122** Ecclesiasticus 28.14–end *or* Ezekiel 36.16–36 John 14.15–end	Psalm **118** 2 Kings 20 Philippians 4.2–end

or, if All Saints' Day is celebrated on Sunday 3 November only:
1st EP of All Saints' Day:
Psalms 1, 5; Ecclesiasticus 44.1–15 *or* Isaiah 40.27–end;
Revelation 19.6–10

			Principal Service	**3rd Service**	**2nd Service**
Sunday	3 November **All Saints' Day**	*Gold or W*	Daniel 7.1–3, 15–18 Psalm 149 Ephesians 1.11–end Luke 6.20–31	MP Psalms 15, 84, 149 Isaiah 35.1–9 Luke 9.18–27	EP Psalms 148, 150 Isaiah 65.17–end Hebrews 11.32—12.2

4 before Advent

		Holy Communion	Morning Prayer	Evening Prayer
Monday	**4 November** R/G DEL week 31	Romans 11.29–end Psalm 69.31–37 Luke 14.12–14	Psalms **2**, 146 or 123, 124, 125, **126** Isaiah 1.1–20 Matthew 1.18–end	Psalms **92**, 96, 97 or **127**, 128, 129 Daniel 1 Revelation 1
Tuesday	**5 November** R/G	Romans 12.5–16 Psalm 131 Luke 14.15–24	Psalms 5, 147.1–12 or **132**, 133 Isaiah 1.21–end Matthew 2.1–15	Psalms 98, 99, **100** or (134,) **135** Daniel 2.1–24 Revelation 2.1–11
Wednesday	**6 November** R/G Leonard, hermit, 6th cent. William Temple, archbishop, teacher of the faith, 1944	Romans 13.8–10 Psalm 112 Luke 14.25–33	Psalms **9**, 147.13–end or **119.153–end** Isaiah 2.1–11 Matthew 2.16–end	Psalms 111, **112**, 116 or **136** Daniel 2.25–end Revelation 2.12–end
Thursday	**7 November** Rw/Gw Willibrord, bishop, 739 (see p.80)	Romans 14.7–12 Psalm 27.14–end Luke 15.1–10	Psalms 11, **15**, 148 or **143**, 146 Isaiah 2.12–end Matthew 3	Psalm **118** or **138**, 140, 141 Daniel 3.1–18 Revelation 3.1–13
Friday	**8 November** Rw/Gw Saints and martyrs of England	Romans 15.14–21 Psalm 98 Luke 16.1–8 *Lesser Festival eucharistic lectionary:* Isaiah 61.4–9 or Ecclesiasticus 44.1–15 Psalm 15 Revelation 19.5–10 John 17.18–23	Psalms **16**, 149 or 142, **144** Isaiah 3.1–15 Matthew 4.1–11	Psalms 137, 138, **143** or **145** Daniel 3.19–end Revelation 3.14–end
Saturday	**9 November** R/G Margery Kempe, mystic, c.1440	Romans 16.3–9, 16, 22–end Psalm 145.1–7 Luke 16.9–15	Psalms **18.31–end**, 150 or **147** Isaiah 4.2—5.7 Matthew 4.12–22	Psalm **145** or **148**, 149, 150 Daniel 4.1–18 Revelation 4

3 before Advent

		Principal Service	3rd Service	2nd Service
Sunday	**10 November** R/G **3rd Sunday before Advent** *Remembrance Sunday*	Job 19.23–27a Psalm 17.1–9 [or 17.1–8] 2 Thessalonians 2.1–5, 13–end Luke 20.27–38	Psalms 20, 90 Isaiah 2.1–5 James 3.13–end	Psalm 40 1 Kings 3.1–15 Romans 8.31–end HC Matthew 22.15–22
		Holy Communion	**Morning Prayer**	**Evening Prayer**
Monday	**11 November** Rw/Gw Martin, bishop, c.397 (see p.79) DEL week 32	Wisdom 1.1–7 or Titus 1.1–9 Psalm 139.1–9 or 24.1–6 Luke 17.1–6	Psalms 19, **20** or 1, 2, 3 Isaiah 5.8–24 Matthew 4.23—5.12	Psalm **34** or **4**, 7 Daniel 4.19–end Revelation 5
Tuesday	**12 November** R/G	Wisdom 2.23—3.9 or Titus 2.1–8, 11–14 Psalm 34.1–6 or 37.3–5, 30–32 Luke 17.7–10	Psalms **21**, 24 or **5**, 6 (8) Isaiah 5.25–end Matthew 5.13–20	Psalms 36, **40** or **9**, 10* Daniel 5.1–12 Revelation 6
Wednesday	**13 November** Rw/Gw Charles Simeon, priest, evangelical divine, 1836 (see p.79)	Wisdom 6.1–11 or Titus 3.1–7 Psalm 82 or 23 Luke 17.11–19	Psalms **23**, 25 or 119.1–32 Isaiah 6 Matthew 5.21–37	Psalm **37** or **11**, 12, 13 Daniel 5.13–end Revelation 7.1–4, 9–end
Thursday	**14 November** R/G *Samuel Seabury, bishop, 1796*	Wisdom 7.22—8.1 or Philemon 7–20 Psalm 119.89–96 or 146.4–end Luke 17.20–25	Psalms **26**, 27 or 14, **15**, 16 Isaiah 7.1–17 Matthew 5.38–end	Psalms 42, **43** or **18*** Daniel 6 Revelation 8
Friday	**15 November** R/G	Wisdom 13.1–9 or 2 John 4–9 Psalm 19.1–4 or 119.1–8 Luke 17.26–end	Psalms 28, **32** or 17, **19** Isaiah 8.1–15 Matthew 6.1–18	Psalm **31** or **22** Daniel 7.1–14 Revelation 9.1–12
Saturday	**16 November** Rw/Gw Margaret, queen, philanthropist, 1093 (see p.81) *Edmund Rich, archbishop, 1240*	Wisdom 18.14–16, 19.6–9 or 3 John 5–8 Psalm 105.1–5, 35–42 or 112 Luke 18.1–8	Psalm **33** or 20, 21, **23** Isaiah 8.16—9.7 Matthew 6.19–end	Psalms 84, **86** or **24**, 25 Daniel 7.15–end Revelation 9.13–end

2 before Advent

		Principal Service	3rd Service	2nd Service
Sunday	**17 November** R/G **2nd Sunday before Advent**	Malachi 4.1–2a Psalm 98 2 Thessalonians 3.6–13 Luke 21.5–19	Psalm 132 1 Samuel 16.1–13 Matthew 13.44–52	Psalms [93] 97 Daniel 6 Matthew 13.1–9, 18–23
		Holy Communion	**Morning Prayer**	**Evening Prayer**
Monday	**18 November** Rw/Gw Elizabeth, princess, philanthropist, 1231 (see p.81) DEL week 33	1 Maccabees 1.10–15, 41–43, 54–57, 62–64 or Revelation 1.1–4, 2.1–5 Psalm 79.1–5 or 1 Luke 18.35–end	Psalms 46, **47** or 27, **30** Isaiah 9.8—10.4 Matthew 7.1–12	Psalms 70, **71** or 26, **28**, 29 Daniel 8.1–14 Revelation 10
Tuesday	**19 November** Rw/Gw Hilda, abbess, 680 (see p.80) *Mechtild, béguine, mystic, 1280*	2 Maccabees 6.18–end or Revelation 3.1–6, 14–31 Psalm 11 or 15 Luke 19.1–10	Psalms 48, **52** or 32, **36** Isaiah 10.5–19 Matthew 7.13–end	Psalms **67**, 72 or **33** Daniel 8.15–end Revelation 11.1–14
Wednesday	**20 November** R/Gr Edmund, king, martyr, 870 (see p.77) *Priscilla Lydia Sellon, a restorer of the religious life in the Church of England, 1876*	2 Maccabees 7.1, 20–31 or Revelation 4 Psalm 116.10–end or 150 Luke 19.11–28	Psalms **56**, 57 or **34** Isaiah 10.20–32 Matthew 8.1–13	Psalm **73** or 1**19.33–56** Daniel 9.1–19 Revelation 11.15–end
Thursday	**21 November** R/G	1 Maccabees 2.15–29 or Revelation 5.1–10 Psalm 129 or 149.1–5 Luke 19.41–44	Psalms 61, **62** or **37*** Isaiah 10.33—11.9 Matthew 8.14–22	Psalms 74, **76** or 39, **40** Daniel 9.20–end Revelation 12
Friday	**22 November** R/G *Cecilia, martyr, c.230*	1 Maccabees 4.36–37, 52–59 or Revelation 10.8–11 Psalm 122 or 119.65–72 Luke 19.45–48	Psalms **63**, 65 or **31** Isaiah 11.10–end of 12 Matthew 8.23–end	Psalm **77** or **35** Daniel 10.1—11.1 Revelation 13.1–10
Saturday	**23 November** R/Gr Clement, bishop, martyr, c.100 (see p.77)	1 Maccabees 6.1–13 or Revelation 11.4–12 Psalm 124 or 144.1–9 Luke 20.27–40	Psalm 78.1–39 or 41, **42**, 43 Isaiah 13.1–13 Matthew 9.1–17	Psalm 78.**40–end** or 45, **46** Daniel 12 Revelation 13.11–end or: 1st EP of Christ the King: Psalms 99, 100; Isaiah 10.33—11.9; 1 Timothy 6.11–16

Christ the King / Sunday next before Advent

		Principal Service	3rd Service	2nd Service
Sunday	**24 November** R/W Christ the King Sunday next before Advent	Jeremiah 23.1–6 Psalm 46 Colossians 1.11–20 Luke 23.33–43	MP Psalms 29, 110 Zechariah 6.9–end Revelation 11.15–18	EP Psalm 72 [or 72.1–7] 1 Samuel 8.4–20 John 18.33–37
		Holy Communion	**Morning Prayer**	**Evening Prayer**
Monday	**25 November** R/G Catherine, martyr, 4th cent. Isaac Watts, hymn writer, 1748 DEL week 34	Daniel 1.1–6, 8–20 Canticle: Bless the Lord Luke 21.1–4	Psalms 92, **96** or **44** Isaiah 14.3–20 Matthew 9.18–34	Psalms **80**, 81 or **47**, 49 Isaiah 40.1–11 Revelation 14.1–13
Tuesday	**26 November** R/G	Daniel 2.31–45 Canticle: Benedicite 1–3 Luke 21.5–11	Psalms **97**, 98, 100 or **48**, 52 Isaiah 17 Matthew 9.35—10.15	Psalms 99, **101** or **50** Isaiah 40.12–26 Revelation 14.14—end of 15
Wednesday	**27 November** R/G	Daniel 5.1–6, 13–14, 16–17, 23–28 Canticle: Benedicite 4–5 Luke 21.12–19	Psalms 110, **111**, **112** or **119.57–80** Isaiah 19 Matthew 10.16–33	Psalms 121, **122**, 123, 124 or **59**, 60 (67) Isaiah 40.27—41.7 Revelation 16.1–11
Thursday	**28 November** R/G	Daniel 6.12–end Canticle: Benedicite 6–8a Luke 21.20–28	Psalms **125**, 126, 127, 128 or 56, **57** (63*) Isaiah 21.1–12 Matthew 10.34—11.1	Psalms 131, 132, **133** or 61, **62**, 64 Isaiah 41.8–20 Revelation 16.12–end
Friday	**29 November** R/G Day of Intercession and Thanksgiving for the missionary work of the Church	Daniel 7.2–14 Canticle: Benedicite 8b–10a Luke 21.29–33	Psalm **139** or **51**, 54 Isaiah 22.1–14 Matthew 11.2–19	Psalms **146**, 147 or **38** Isaiah 41.21—42.9 Revelation 17 or: 1st EP of Andrew the Apostle: Psalm 48; Isaiah 49.1–9a; 1 Corinthians 4.9–16
		Principal Service	**3rd Service**	**2nd Service**
Saturday	**30 November** R Andrew the Apostle	Isaiah 52.7–10 Psalm 19.1–6 Romans 10.12–18 Matthew 4.18–22	MP Psalms 47, 147.1–12 Ezekiel 47.1–12 or Ecclesiasticus 14.20–end John 12.20–32	EP Psalms 87, 96 Zechariah 8.20–end John 1.35–42

¶ Additional Weekday Lectionary

This Additional Weekday Lectionary provides two readings for each day of the year, except for Sundays, Principal Feasts and other Principal Holy Days, Holy Week and Festivals (for which the readings provided in the main body of this lectionary are used). The readings for 'first evensongs' in the main body of the lectionary are used on the eves of Principal Feasts and may be used on the eves of Festivals. This lectionary is intended particularly for use in those places of worship that attract occasional rather than daily worshippers, and can be used either at Morning or Evening Prayer. Psalmody is not provided and should be taken from the daily provision earlier in this volume.

2 December – Advent 1

Monday	3 December	Malachi 3.1–6	Matthew 3.1–6
Tuesday	4 December	Zephaniah 3.14–end	1 Thessalonians 4.13–end
Wednesday	5 December	Isaiah 65.17—66.2	Matthew 24.1–14
Thursday	6 December	Micah 5.2–5a	John 3.16–21
Friday	7 December	Isaiah 66.18–end	Luke 13.22–30
Saturday	8 December	Micah 7.8–15	Romans 15.30—16.7, 25–end

9 December – Advent 2

Monday	10 December	Jeremiah 7.1–11	Philippians 4.4–9
Tuesday	11 December	Daniel 7.9–14	Matthew 24.15–28
Wednesday	12 December	Amos 9.11–end	Romans 13.8–end
Thursday	13 December	Jeremiah 23.5–8	Mark 11.1–11
Friday	14 December	Jeremiah 33.14–22	Luke 21.25–36
Saturday	15 December	Zechariah 14.4–11	Revelation 22.1–7

16 December – Advent 3

Monday	17 December	Ecclesiasticus 24.1–9 or Proverbs 8.22–31	1 Corinthians 2.1–13
Tuesday	18 December	Exodus 3.1–6	Acts 7.20–36
Wednesday	19 December	Isaiah 11.1–9	Romans 15.7–13
Thursday	20 December	Isaiah 22.21–23	Revelation 3.7–13
Friday	21 December	Numbers 24.15b–19	Revelation 22.10–21
Saturday	22 December	Jeremiah 30.7–11a	Acts 4.1–12

23 December – Advent 4

Monday	24 December	At Evening Prayer the readings for Christmas Eve are used. At other services, the following readings are used:	
		Isaiah 29.13–18	1 John 4.7–16
Tuesday	25 December	**Christmas Day** – see p.13	
Wednesday	26 December	Stephen, deacon, first martyr – see p.13	
Thursday	27 December	John, Apostle and Evangelist – see p.13	
Friday	28 December	The Holy Innocents – see p.13	
Saturday	29 December	Micah 1.1–4; 2.12–13	Luke 2.1–7

30 December – Christmas 1

Monday	31 December	Ecclesiastes 3.1–13	Revelation 21.1–8
Tuesday	1 January	Naming and Circumcision of Jesus – see p.14	
Wednesday	2 January	Isaiah 66.6–14	Matthew 12.46–50
Thursday	3 January	Deuteronomy 6.4–15	John 10.31–end
Friday	4 January	Isaiah 63.7–16	Galatians 3.23—4.7
Saturday	5 January	At Evening Prayer the readings for the Eve of the Epiphany are used. At other services, the following readings are used:	
		Isaiah 12	2 Corinthians 2.12–end

6 January – The Epiphany

Monday	7 January	Genesis 25.19–end	Ephesians 1.1–6
Tuesday	8 January	Joel 2.28–end	Ephesians 1.7–14
Wednesday	9 January	Proverbs 8.12–21	Ephesians 1.15–end
Thursday	10 January	Genesis 19.15–29	Ephesians 2.1–10
Friday	11 January	Genesis 17.1–14	Ephesians 2.11–end
Saturday	12 January	At Evening Prayer the readings for the Eve of the Baptism of Christ are used.	
		At other services, the following readings are used:	
		1 Kings 10.1–13	Ephesians 3.14–end

13 January – Baptism of Christ (Epiphany 2)

Monday	14 January	Isaiah 41.14–20	John 1.29–34
Tuesday	15 January	Exodus 17.1–7	Acts 8.26–end
Wednesday	16 January	Exodus 15.1–19	Colossians 2.8–15
Thursday	17 January	Zechariah 6.9–15	1 Peter 2.4–10
Friday	18 January	Isaiah 51.7–16	Galatians 6.14–18
Saturday	19 January	Leviticus 16.11–22	Hebrews 10.19–25

20 January – Epiphany 3

Monday	21 January	1 Kings 17.8–16	Mark 8.1–10
Tuesday	22 January	1 Kings 19.1–9a	Mark 1.9–15
Wednesday	23 January	1 Kings 19.9b–18	Mark 9.2–13
Thursday	24 January	Leviticus 11.1–8, 13–19, 41–45	Acts 10.9–16
		or 1st EP of the Conversion of Paul	
Friday	25 January	Conversion of Paul – see p.17	
Saturday	26 January	Genesis 35.1–15	Acts 10.44–end

27 January – Epiphany 4

Monday	28 January	Ezekiel 37.15–end	John 17.1–19
Tuesday	29 January	Ezekiel 20.39–44	John 17.20–end
Wednesday	30 January	Nehemiah 2.1–10	Romans 12.1–8
Thursday	31 January	Deuteronomy 26.16–end	Romans 14.1–9
Friday	1 February	Leviticus 19.9–28	Romans 15.1–7
		If the **Presentation of Christ** is celebrated on Saturday 2 February the readings for the Eve of the Presentation are used at Evening Prayer.	
Saturday	2 February	**Presentation of Christ** – see p.18	
		or, if, for pastoral reasons, the **Presentation of Christ** is celebrated on Sunday 3 February, the readings for the Eve of the Presentation are used at Evening Prayer. At other services, the following readings are used:	
		Jeremiah 33.1–11	1 Peter 5.5b–end

3 February – 5 before Lent / Presentation

Monday	4 February	Isaiah 42.10–21	Luke 1.5–25
Tuesday	5 February	1 Samuel 4.12–end	Luke 1.57–80
Wednesday	6 February	Baruch 5 or Haggai 1.1–11	Mark 1.1–11
Thursday	7 February	Isaiah 35	Matthew 11.2–19
Friday	8 February	2 Samuel 11.1–17	Matthew 14.1–12
Saturday	9 February	Isaiah 43.15–21	Acts 19.1–10

10 February – 4 before Lent

Monday	11 February	Genesis 1.26–end	Mark 10.1–16
Tuesday	12 February	Ruth 1.1–18	1 John 3.14–end
Wednesday	13 February	1 Samuel 1.19b–end	Luke 2.41–end
Thursday	14 February	Genesis 47.1–12	Ephesians 3.14–end
Friday	15 February	2 Samuel 1.17–end	Romans 8.28–end
Saturday	16 February	Song of Solomon 2.8–end	1 Corinthians 13

17 February – 3 before Lent

Monday	18 February	Exodus 23.1–13	James 2.1–13
Tuesday	19 February	Deuteronomy 10.12–end	Hebrews 13.1–16
Wednesday	20 February	Isaiah 58.6–end	Matthew 25.31–end
Thursday	21 February	Isaiah 42.1–9	Luke 4.14–21
Friday	22 February	Amos 5.6–15	Ephesians 4.25–end
Saturday	23 February	Amos 5.18–24	John 2.13–22

Additional Weekday Lectionary

		24 February – 2 before Lent	
Monday	25 February	Isaiah 61.1–9	Mark 6.1–13
Tuesday	26 February	Isaiah 52.1–10	Romans 10.5–21
Wednesday	27 February	Isaiah 52.13—53.6	Romans 15.14–21
Thursday	28 February	Isaiah 53.4–12	2 Corinthians 4.1–10
Friday	1 March	Zechariah 8.16–end	Matthew 10.1–15
Saturday	2 March	Jeremiah 1.4–10	Matthew 10.16–22
		3 March – Sunday next before Lent	
Monday	4 March	2 Kings 2.13–22	3 John
Tuesday	5 March	Judges 14.5–17	Revelation 10.4–11
Wednesday	6 March	**Ash Wednesday** – see p.23	
Thursday	7 March	Genesis 2.7–end	Hebrews 2.5–end
Friday	8 March	Genesis 4.1–12	Hebrews 4.12–end
Saturday	9 March	2 Kings 22.11–end	Hebrews 5.1–10
		10 March – Lent 1	
Monday	11 March	Genesis 6.11–end, 7.11–16	Luke 4.14–21
Tuesday	12 March	Deuteronomy 31.7–13	1 John 3.1–10
Wednesday	13 March	Genesis 11.1–9	Matthew 24.15–28
Thursday	14 March	Genesis 13.1–13	1 Peter 2.13–end
Friday	15 March	Genesis 21.1–8	Luke 9.18–27
Saturday	16 March	Genesis 32.22–32	2 Peter 1.10–end
		17 March – Lent 2	
Monday	18 March	1 Chronicles 21.1–17 or 1st EP of Joseph of Nazareth	1 John 2.1–8
Tuesday	19 March	**Joseph of Nazareth** – see p.25	
Wednesday	20 March	Job 1.1–22	Luke 21.34—22.6
Thursday	21 March	2 Chronicles 29.1–11	Mark 11.15–19
Friday	22 March	Exodus 19.1–9*a*	1 Peter 1.1–9
Saturday	23 March	Exodus 19.9*b*–19	Acts 7.44–50
		24 March – Lent 3	
Monday	25 March	**Annunciation of Our Lord to the Blessed Virgin Mary** – see p.26	
Tuesday	26 March	Exodus 15.22–27	Hebrews 10.32–end
Wednesday	27 March	Genesis 9.8–17	1 Peter 3.18–end
Thursday	28 March	Daniel 12.5–end	Mark 13.21–end
Friday	29 March	Numbers 20.1–13	1 Corinthians 10.23–end
Saturday	30 March	Isaiah 43.14–end	Hebrews 3.1–15
		31 March – Lent 4	
Monday	1 April	2 Kings 24.18—25.7	1 Corinthians 15.20–34
Tuesday	2 April	Jeremiah 13.12–19	Acts 13.26–35
Wednesday	3 April	Jeremiah 13.20–27	1 Peter 1.17—2.3
Thursday	4 April	Jeremiah 22.11–19	Luke 11.37–52
Friday	5 April	Jeremiah 17.1–14	Luke 6.17–26
Saturday	6 April	Ezra 1	2 Corinthians 1.12–19
		7 April – Lent 5	
Monday	8 April	Joel 2.12–17	2 John
Tuesday	9 April	Isaiah 58.1–14	Mark 10.32–45
Wednesday	10 April	Job 36.1–12	John 14.1–14
Thursday	11 April	Jeremiah 9.17–22	Luke 13.31–35
Friday	12 April	Lamentations 5.1–3, 19–22	John 12.20–26
Saturday	13 April	Job 17.6–end	John 12.27–36
		From the Monday of Holy Week until Easter Eve the seasonal lectionary is used: see pp.29–30.	
		21 April – Easter	
Monday	22 April	Isaiah 54.1–14	Romans 1.1–7
Tuesday	23 April	Isaiah 51.1–11	John 5.19–29
Wednesday	24 April	Isaiah 26.1–19	John 20.1–10
Thursday	25 April	Isaiah 43.14–21	Revelation 1.4–end
Friday	26 April	Isaiah 42.10–17	1 Thessalonians 5.1–11
Saturday	27 April	Job 14.1–14	John 21.1–14

		28 April – Easter 2	
Monday	29 April	George, Martyr, Patron of England transferred – see p.32	
Tuesday	30 April	Mark the Evangelist transferred – see p.32	
Wednesday	1 May	Philip and James, Apostles – see p.32	
Thursday	2 May	Jonah 2	Mark 4.35–end
Friday	3 May	Genesis 6.9–end	1 Peter 3.8–end
Saturday	4 May	1 Samuel 2.1–8	Matthew 28.8–15
		5 May – Easter 3	
Monday	6 May	Exodus 24.1–11	Revelation 5
Tuesday	7 May	Leviticus 19.9–18, 32–end	Matthew 5.38–end
Wednesday	8 May	Genesis 3.8–21	1 Corinthians 15.12–28
Thursday	9 May	Isaiah 33.13–22	Mark 6.47–end
Friday	10 May	Nehemiah 9.6–17	Romans 5.12–end
Saturday	11 May	Isaiah 61.10—62.5	Luke 24.1–12
		12 May – Easter 4	
Monday	13 May	Jeremiah 31.10–17	Revelation 7.9–end
		or 1st EP of Matthias the Apostle	
Tuesday	14 May	Matthias the Apostle – see p.34	
Wednesday	15 May	Genesis 2.4b–9	1 Corinthians 15.35–49
Thursday	16 May	Proverbs 28.3–end	Mark 10.17–31
Friday	17 May	Ecclesiastes 12.1–8	Romans 6.1–11
Saturday	18 May	1 Chronicles 29.10–13	Luke 24.13–35
		19 May – Easter 5	
Monday	20 May	Genesis 15.1–18	Romans 4.13–end
Tuesday	21 May	Deuteronomy 8.1–10	Matthew 6.19–end
Wednesday	22 May	Hosea 13.4–14	1 Corinthians 15.50–end
Thursday	23 May	Exodus 3.1–15	Mark 12.18–27
Friday	24 May	Ezekiel 36.33–end	Romans 8.1–11
Saturday	25 May	Isaiah 38.9–20	Luke 24.33–end
		26 May – Easter 6	
Monday	27 May	Proverbs 4.1–13	Philippians 2.1–11
Tuesday	28 May	Isaiah 32.12–end	Romans 5.1–11
Wednesday	29 May	At Evening Prayer the readings for the Eve of Ascension Day are used.	
		At other services, the following readings are used:	
		Isaiah 43.1–13	Titus 2.11—3.8
Thursday	30 May	**Ascension Day** – see p.37	
Friday	31 May	Visit of the Blessed Virgin Mary to Elizabeth – see p.37	
Saturday	1 June	Numbers 11.16–17, 24–29	1 Corinthians 2
		2 June – Easter 7	
Monday	3 June	Numbers 27.15–end	1 Corinthians 3
Tuesday	4 June	1 Samuel 10.1–10	1 Corinthians 12.1–13
Wednesday	5 June	1 Kings 19.1–18	Matthew 3.13–end
Thursday	6 June	Ezekiel 11.14–20	Matthew 9.35—10.20
Friday	7 June	Ezekiel 36.22–28	Matthew 12.22–32
Saturday	8 June	At Evening Prayer the readings for the Eve of Pentecost are used.	
		At other services, the following readings are used:	
		Micah 3.1–8	Ephesians 6.10–20
		9 June – Pentecost	
Monday	10 June	Genesis 12.1–9	Romans 4.13–end
		or 1st EP of Barnabas the Apostle	
Tuesday	11 June	Barnabas the Apostle – see p.39	
Wednesday	12 June	Genesis 15	Romans 4.1–8
Thursday	13 June	Genesis 22.1–18	Hebrews 11.8–19
Friday	14 June	Isaiah 51.1–8	John 8.48–end
Saturday	15 June	At Evening Prayer the readings for the Eve of Trinity Sunday are used.	
		At other services, the following readings are used:	
		Ecclesiasticus 44.19–23	James 2.14–26
		or Joshua 2.1–15	

		16 June – Trinity Sunday	
Monday	17 June	Exodus 2.1–10	Hebrews 11.23–31
Tuesday	18 June	Exodus 2.11–end	Acts 7.17–29
Wednesday	19 June	Exodus 3.1–12	Acts 7.30–38
		or 1st EP of Corpus Christi	
Thursday	20 June	*Day of Thanksgiving for the Institution of Holy Communion (Corpus Christi) – see p.40*	
		or, where Corpus Christi *is not celebrated as a Festival:*	
		Exodus 6.1–13	John 9.24–38
Friday	21 June	Exodus 34.1–10	Mark 7.1–13
Saturday	22 June	Exodus 34.27–end	2 Corinthians 3.7–end
		23 June – Trinity 1	
Monday	24 June	*Birth of John the Baptist – see p.41*	
Tuesday	25 June	Genesis 41.15–40	Mark 13.1–13
Wednesday	26 June	Genesis 42.17–end	Matthew 18.1–14
Thursday	27 June	Genesis 45.1–15	Acts 7.9–16
Friday	28 June	Genesis 47.1–12	1 Thessalonians 5.12–end
		or 1st EP of Peter and Paul, Apostles (*or* Peter the Apostle)	
Saturday	29 June	*Peter and Paul, Apostles (or Peter the Apostle) – see p.41*	
		30 June – Trinity 2	
Monday	1 July	Isaiah 32	James 3.13–end
Tuesday	2 July	Proverbs 3.1–18	Matthew 5.1–12
		or 1st EP of Thomas the Apostle	
Wednesday	3 July	*Thomas the Apostle – see p.42*	
Thursday	4 July	Jeremiah 6.9–15	1 Timothy 2.1–6
Friday	5 July	1 Samuel 16.14–end	John 14.15–end
Saturday	6 July	Isaiah 6.1–9	Revelation 19.9–end
		7 July – Trinity 3	
Monday	8 July	Exodus 13.13*b*–end	Luke 15.1–10
Tuesday	9 July	Proverbs 1.20–end	James 5.13–end
Wednesday	10 July	Isaiah 5.8–24	James 1.17–25
Thursday	11 July	Isaiah 57.14–end	John 13.1–17
Friday	12 July	Jeremiah 15.15–end	Luke 16.19–31
Saturday	13 July	Isaiah 25.1–9	Acts 2.22–33
		14 July – Trinity 4	
Monday	15 July	Exodus 20.1–17	Matthew 6.1–15
Tuesday	16 July	Proverbs 6.6–19	Luke 4.1–14
Wednesday	17 July	Isaiah 24.1–15	1 Corinthians 6.1–11
Thursday	18 July	Job 7	Matthew 7.21–29
Friday	19 July	Jeremiah 20.7–end	Matthew 27.27–44
Saturday	20 July	Job 28	Hebrews 11.32—12.2
		21 July – Trinity 5	
Monday	22 July	*Mary Magdalene – see p.45*	
Tuesday	23 July	Proverbs 9.1–12	2 Thessalonians 2.13—3.5
Wednesday	24 July	Isaiah 26.1–9	Romans 8.12–27
		or 1st EP of James the Apostle	
Thursday	25 July	*James the Apostle – see p.45*	
Friday	26 July	2 Samuel 5.1–12	Matthew 27.45–56
Saturday	27 July	Hosea 11.1–11	Matthew 28.1–7
		28 July – Trinity 6	
Monday	29 July	Exodus 40.1–16	Luke 14.15–24
Tuesday	30 July	Proverbs 11.1–12	Mark 12.38–44
Wednesday	31 July	Isaiah 33.2–10	Philippians 1.1–11
Thursday	1 August	Job 38	Luke 18.1–14
Friday	2 August	Job 42.1–6	John 3.1–15
Saturday	3 August	Ecclesiastes 9.1–11	Hebrews 1.1–9

4 August – Trinity 7

Monday	5 August	Numbers 23.1–12 *or* 1st EP of the Transfiguration	1 Corinthians 1.10–17
Tuesday	6 August	The Transfiguration of Our Lord – see p.47	
Wednesday	7 August	Isaiah 49.8–13	2 Corinthians 8.1–11
Thursday	8 August	Hosea 14	John 15.1–17
Friday	9 August	2 Samuel 18.18–end	Matthew 27.57–66
Saturday	10 August	Isaiah 55.1–7	Mark 16.1–8

11 August – Trinity 8

Monday	12 August	Joel 3.16–21	Mark 4.21–34
Tuesday	13 August	Proverbs 12.13–end	John 1.43–51
Wednesday	14 August	Isaiah 55.8–end *or* 1st EP of The Blessed Virgin Mary	2 Timothy 2.8–19
Thursday	15 August	The Blessed Virgin Mary – see p.48	
Friday	16 August	Jeremiah 14.1–9	Luke 8.4–15
Saturday	17 August	Ecclesiastes 5.10–19	1 Timothy 6.6–16

18 August – Trinity 9

Monday	19 August	Joshua 1.1–9	1 Corinthians 9.19–end
Tuesday	20 August	Proverbs 15.1–11	Galatians 2.15–end
Wednesday	21 August	Isaiah 49.1–7	1 John 1
Thursday	22 August	Proverbs 27.1–12	John 15.12–27
Friday	23 August	Isaiah 59.8–end *or* 1st EP of Bartholomew the Apostle	Mark 15.6–20
Saturday	24 August	Bartholomew the Apostle – see p.49	

25 August – Trinity 10

Monday	26 August	Judges 13.1–23	Luke 10.38–42
Tuesday	27 August	Proverbs 15.15–end	Matthew 15.21–28
Wednesday	28 August	Isaiah 45.1–7	Ephesians 4.1–16
Thursday	29 August	Jeremiah 16.1–15	Luke 12.35–48
Friday	30 August	Jeremiah 18.1–11	Hebrews 1.1–9
Saturday	31 August	Jeremiah 26.1–19	Ephesians 3.1–13

1 September – Trinity 11

Monday	2 September	Ruth 2.1–13	Luke 10.25–37
Tuesday	3 September	Proverbs 16.1–11	Philippians 3.4b–end
Wednesday	4 September	Deuteronomy 11.1–21	2 Corinthians 9.6–end
Thursday	5 September	Ecclesiasticus 2 *or* Ecclesiastes 2.12–25	John 16.1–15
Friday	6 September	Obadiah 1–10	John 19.1–16
Saturday	7 September	2 Kings 2.11–14	Luke 24.36–end

8 September – Trinity 12

Monday	9 September	1 Samuel 17.32–50	Matthew 8.14–22
Tuesday	10 September	Proverbs 17.1–15	Luke 7.1–17
Wednesday	11 September	Jeremiah 5.20–end	2 Peter 3.8–end
Thursday	12 September	Daniel 2.1–23	Luke 10.1–20
Friday	13 September	Daniel 3.1–28 *or* 1st EP of Holy Cross Day	Revelation 15
Saturday	14 September	Holy Cross Day – see p.52	

15 September – Trinity 13

Monday	16 September	2 Samuel 7.4–17	2 Corinthians 5.1–10
Tuesday	17 September	Proverbs 18.10–21	Romans 14.10–end
Wednesday	18 September	Judges 4.1–10	Romans 1.8–17
Thursday	19 September	Isaiah 49.14–end	John 16.16–24
Friday	20 September	Job 9.1–24 *or* 1st EP of Matthew, Apostle and Evangelist	Mark 15.21–32
Saturday	21 September	Matthew, Apostle and Evangelist – see p.53	

22 September – Trinity 14

Day	Date	Reading 1	Reading 2
Monday	23 September	Haggai 1	Mark 7.9–23
Tuesday	24 September	Proverbs 21.1–18	Mark 6.30–44
Wednesday	25 September	Hosea 11.1–11	1 John 4.9–end
Thursday	26 September	Lamentations 3.34–48	Romans 7.14–end
Friday	27 September	1 Kings 19.4–18	1 Thessalonians 3
Saturday	28 September	Ecclesiasticus 4.11–28 *or* Deuteronomy 29.2–15	2 Timothy 3.10–end

29 September – Michael and All Angels / Trinity 15

Day	Date	Reading 1	Reading 2
Monday	30 September	Wisdom 6.12–21 *or* Job 12.1–16 *or* **Michael and All Angels** transferred (see p.55)	Matthew 15.1–9
Tuesday	1 October	Proverbs 8.1–11	Luke 6.39–end
Wednesday	2 October	Proverbs 2.1–15	Colossians 1.9–20
Thursday	3 October	Baruch 3.14–end *or* Genesis 1.1–13	John 1.1–18
Friday	4 October	Ecclesiasticus 1.1–20 *or* Deuteronomy 7.7–16	1 Corinthians 1.18–end
Saturday	5 October	Wisdom 9.1–12 *or* Jeremiah 1.4–10	Luke 2.41–end

6 October – Trinity 16

Day	Date	Reading 1	Reading 2
Monday	7 October	Genesis 21.1–13	Luke 1.26–38
Tuesday	8 October	Ruth 4.7–17	Luke 2.25–38
Wednesday	9 October	2 Kings 4.1–7	John 2.1–11
Thursday	10 October	2 Kings 4.25b–37	Mark 3.19b–35
Friday	11 October	Judith 8.9–17, 28–36 *or* Ruth 1.1–18	John 19.25b–30
Saturday	12 October	Exodus 15.19–27	Acts 1.6–14

13 October – Trinity 17

Day	Date	Reading 1	Reading 2
Monday	14 October	Exodus 19.16–end	Hebrews 12.18–end
Tuesday	15 October	1 Chronicles 16.1–13	Revelation 11.15–end
Wednesday	16 October	1 Chronicles 29.10–19	Colossians 3.12–17
Thursday	17 October	Nehemiah 8.1–12 *or* 1st EP of Luke the Evangelist	1 Corinthians 14.1–12
Friday	18 October	**Luke the Evangelist** – see p.58	
Saturday	19 October	Daniel 6.6–23	Revelation 12.7–12

20 October – Trinity 18

Day	Date	Reading 1	Reading 2
Monday	21 October	2 Samuel 22.4–7, 17–20	Hebrews 7.26—8.6
Tuesday	22 October	Proverbs 22.17–end	2 Corinthians 12.1–10
Wednesday	23 October	Hosea 14	James 2.14–26
Thursday	24 October	Isaiah 24.1–15	John 16.25–33
Friday	25 October	Jeremiah 14.1–9	Luke 23.44–56
Saturday	26 October	Zechariah 8.14–end	John 20.19–end

27 October – Last after Trinity

Day	Date	Reading 1	Reading 2
Monday	28 October	**Simon and Jude, Apostles** – see p.60	
Tuesday	29 October	1 Samuel 4.12–end	Luke 1.57–80
Wednesday	30 October	Baruch 5 *or* Haggai 1.1–11	Mark 1.1–11
Thursday	31 October	Isaiah 35 *or* 1st EP of All Saints' Day	Matthew 11.2–19
Friday	1 November	**All Saints' Day** – see p.61 *or,* if **All Saints' Day** is celebrated on Sunday 3 November only, the following readings are used: 2 Samuel 11.1–17	Matthew 14.1–12
Saturday	2 November	Isaiah 43.15–21 *or* 1st EP of **All Saints' Day**, if All Saints' Day is celebrated on 3 November.	Acts 19.1–10

3 November – 4 before Advent / All Saints' Day

Day	Date	Reading 1	Reading 2
Monday	4 November	Esther 3.1–11, 4.7–17	Matthew 18.1–10
Tuesday	5 November	Ezekiel 18.21–end	Matthew 18.12–20
Wednesday	6 November	Proverbs 3.27–end	Matthew 18.21–end
Thursday	7 November	Exodus 23.1–9	Matthew 19.1–15
Friday	8 November	Proverbs 3.13–18	Matthew 19.16–end
Saturday	9 November	Deuteronomy 28.1–6	Matthew 20.1–16

10 November – 3 before Advent (Remembrance Sunday)

Monday	11 November	Isaiah 40.21–end	Romans 11.25–end
Tuesday	12 November	Ezekiel 34.20–end	John 10.1–18
Wednesday	13 November	Leviticus 26.3–13	Titus 2.1–10
Thursday	14 November	Hosea 6.1–6	Matthew 9.9–13
Friday	15 November	Malachi 4	John 4.5–26
Saturday	16 November	Micah 6.6–8	Colossians 3.12–17

17 November – 2 before Advent

Monday	18 November	Micah 7.1–7	Matthew 10.24–39
Tuesday	19 November	Habakkuk 3.1–19*a*	1 Corinthians 4.9–16
Wednesday	20 November	Zechariah 8.1–13	Mark 13.3–8
Thursday	21 November	Zechariah 10.6–end	1 Peter 5.1–11
Friday	22 November	Micah 4.1–5	Luke 9.28–36
Saturday	23 November	At Evening Prayer the readings for the Eve of Christ the King are used. At other services, the following readings are used: Exodus 16.1–21	John 6.3–15

24 November – Christ the King (Sunday next before Advent)

Monday	25 November	Jeremiah 30.1–3, 10–17	Romans 12.9–21
Tuesday	26 November	Jeremiah 30.18–24	John 10.22–30
Wednesday	27 November	Jeremiah 31.1–9	Matthew 15.21–31
Thursday	28 November	Jeremiah 31.10–17	Matthew 16.13–end
Friday	29 November	Jeremiah 31.31–37 or 1st EP of Andrew the Apostle	Hebrews 10.11–18
Saturday	30 November	Andrew the Apostle – see p.66	

¶ Collects and Post Communions

All the contemporary language Collects and Post Communions, including the Additional Collects, may be found in *Common Worship: Collects and Post Communions* (Church House Publishing: London, 2004). The Additional Collects are also published separately.

The contemporary language Collects and Post Communions all appear in *Times and Seasons: President's Edition for Holy Communion*. Apart from the Additional Collects, they appear in the other Common Worship volumes as follows:

¶ President's edition: all Collects and Post Communions;
¶ *Daily Prayer*: all Collects;
¶ main volume: Collects and Post Communions for Sundays, Principal Feasts and Holy Days, and Festivals;
¶ *Festivals*: Collects and Post Communions for Festivals, Lesser Festivals, Common of the Saints and Special Occasions.

The traditional-language Collects and Post Communions all appear in the president's edition. They appear in other publications as follows:

¶ main volume: Collects and Post Communions for Sundays, Principal Feasts and Holy Days, and Festivals;
¶ separate booklet: Collects and Post Communions for Lesser Festivals, Common of the Saints and Special Occasions.

¶ Lectionary for Dedication Festival

If date not known, observe on the first Sunday in October or Last Sunday after Trinity.

Evening Prayer on the Eve
Psalm 24
2 Chronicles 7.11–16
John 4.19–29

Dedication Festival *Gold or White*

	Principal Service	3rd Service	2nd Service	Psalmody
Year A	1 Kings 8.22–30 *or* Revelation 21.9–14 Psalm 122 Hebrews 12.18–24 Matthew 21.12–16	Haggai 2.6–9 Hebrews 10.19–25	Jeremiah 7.1–11 1 Corinthians 3.9–17 HC Luke 19.1–10	MP 48, 150 EP 132
Year B	Genesis 28.11–18 *or* Revelation 21.9–14 Psalm 122 1 Peter 2.1–10 John 10.22–29	Haggai 2.6–9 Hebrews 10.19–25	Jeremiah 7.1–11 Luke 19.1–10	MP 48, 150 EP 132
Year C	1 Chronicles 29.6–19 Psalm 122 Ephesians 2.19–22 John 2.13–22	Haggai 2.6–9 Hebrews 10.19–25	Jeremiah 7.1–11 Luke 19.1–10	MP 48, 150 EP 132

¶ *Lectionary for Common of the Saints*

The Blessed Virgin Mary

Genesis 3.8–15, 20; Isaiah 7.10–14; Micah 5.1–4
Psalms 45.10–17; 113; 131
Acts 1.12–14; Romans 8.18–30; Galatians 4.4–7
Luke 1.26–38; *or* 1.39–47; John 19.25–27

Martyrs

2 Chronicles 24.17–21; Isaiah 43.1–7; Jeremiah 11.18–20; Wisdom 4.10–15
Psalms 3; 11; 31.1–5; 44.18–24; 126
Romans 8.35–end; 2 Corinthians 4.7–15; 2 Timothy 2.3–7 [8–13]; Hebrews 11.32–end;
    1 Peter 4.12–end; Revelation 12.10–12*a*
Matthew 10.16–22; *or* 10.28–39; *or* 16.24–26; John 12.24–26; *or* 15.18–21

Agnes (21 Jan): *also* Revelation 7.13–end
Alban (22 June): *especially* 2 Timothy 2.3–13; John 12.24–26
Alphege (19 Apr): *also* Hebrews 5.1–4
Boniface (5 June): *also* Acts 20.24–28
Charles (30 Jan): *also* Ecclesiasticus 2.12–end; 1 Timothy 6.12–16
Clement (23 Nov): *also* Philippians 3.17—4.3; Matthew 16.13–19
Cyprian (15 Sept): *especially* 1 Peter 4.12–end; *also* Matthew 18.18–22
Edmund (20 Nov): *also* Proverbs 20.28; 21.1–4, 7
Ignatius (17 Oct): *also* Philippians 3.7–12; John 6.52–58
James Hannington (29 Oct): *especially* Matthew 10.28–39
Janani Luwum (17 Feb): *also* Ecclesiasticus 4.20–28; John 12.24–32
John Coleridge Patteson (20 Sept): *especially* 2 Chronicles 24.17–21; *also* Acts 7.55–end
Justin (1 June): *especially* John 15.18–21; *also* 1 Maccabees 2.15–22; 1 Corinthians 1.18–25
Laurence (10 Aug): *also* 2 Corinthians 9.6–10
Lucy (13 Dec): *also* Wisdom 3.1–7; 2 Corinthians 4.6–15
Oswald (5 Aug): *especially* 1 Peter 4.12–end; John 16.29–end
Perpetua, Felicity and comps (7 Mar): *especially* Revelation 12.10–12*a*; *also* Wisdom 3.1–7
Polycarp (23 Feb): *also* Revelation 2.8–11
Thomas Becket (29 Dec *or* 7 Jul): *especially* Matthew 10.28–33; *also* Ecclesiasticus 51.1–8
William Tyndale (6 Oct): *also* Proverbs 8.4–11; 2 Timothy 3.12–end

Teachers of the Faith and Spiritual Writers

1 Kings 3.[6–10] 11–14; Proverbs 4.1–9; Wisdom 7.7–10, 15–16; Ecclesiasticus 39.1–10
Psalms 19.7–10; 34.11–17; 37.31–35; 119.89–96; 119.97–104
1 Corinthians 1.18–25; *or* 2.1–10; *or* 2.9–end; Ephesians 3.8–12; 2 Timothy 4.1–8; Titus 2.1–8
Matthew 5.13–19; *or* 13.52–end; *or* 23.8–12; Mark 4.1–9; John 16.12–15

Ambrose (7 Dec): *also* Isaiah 41.9b–13; Luke 22.24–30
Anselm (21 Apr): *also* Wisdom 9.13–end; Romans 5.8–11
Athanasius (2 May): *also* Ecclesiasticus 4.20–28; *also* Matthew 10.24–27
Augustine of Hippo (28 Aug): *especially* Ecclesiasticus 39.1–10; *also* Romans 13.11–13
Basil and Gregory (2 Jan): *especially* 2 Timothy 4.1–8; Matthew 5.13–19
Bernard (20 Aug): *especially* Revelation 19.5–9
Catherine of Siena (29 Apr): *also* Proverbs 8.1, 6–11; John 17.12–end
Francis de Sales (24 Jan): *also* Proverbs 3.13–18; John 3.17–21
Gregory the Great (3 Sept): *also* 1 Thessalonians 2.3–8
Gregory of Nyssa and Macrina (19 July): *especially* 1 Corinthians 2.9–13; *also* Wisdom 9.13–17
Hilary (13 Jan): *also* 1 John 2.18–25; John 8.25–32
Irenaeus (28 June): *also* 2 Peter 1.16–end
Jeremy Taylor (13 Aug); *also* Titus 2.7–8, 11–14
John Bunyan (30 Aug): *also* Hebrews 12.1–2; Luke 21.21, 34–36
John Chrysostom (13 Sept): *especially* Matthew 5.13–19; *also* Jeremiah 1.4–10
John of the Cross (14 Dec): *especially* 1 Corinthians 2.1–10; *also* John 14.18–23
Leo (10 Nov): *also* 1 Peter 5.1–11
Richard Hooker (3 Nov): *especially* John 16.12–15; *also* Ecclesiasticus 44.10–15
Teresa of Avila (15 Oct): *also* Romans 8.22–27
Thomas Aquinas (28 Jan): *especially* Wisdom 7.7–10, 15–16; 1 Corinthians 2.9–end; John 16.12–15
William Law (10 Apr): *especially* 1 Corinthians 2.9–end; *also* Matthew 17.1–9

Bishops and Other Pastors

1 Samuel 16.1, 6–13; Isaiah 6.1–8; Jeremiah 1.4–10; Ezekiel 3.16–21; Malachi 2.5–7
Psalms 1; 15; 16.5–end; 96; 110
Acts 20.28–35; 1 Corinthians 4.1–5; 2 Corinthians 4.1–10 [*or* 1–2, 5–7];
    or 5.14–20; 1 Peter 5.1–4
Matthew 11.25–end; *or* 24.42–46; John 10.11–16; *or* 15.9–17; *or* 21.15–17

Augustine of Canterbury (26 May): *also* 1 Thessalonians 2.2b–8; Matthew 13.31–33
Charles Simeon (13 Nov): *especially* Malachi 2.5–7; *also* Colossians 1.3–8; Luke 8.4–8
David (1 Mar): *also* 2 Samuel 23.1–4; Psalm 89.19–22, 24
Dunstan (19 May): *especially* Matthew 24.42–46; *also* Exodus 31.1–5
Edward King (8 Mar): *also* Hebrews 13.1–8
George Herbert (27 Feb): *especially* Malachi 2.5–7; Matthew 11.25–end;
    also Revelation 19.5–9
Hugh (17 Nov); *also* 1 Timothy 6.11–16
John Keble (14 July): *also* Lamentations 3.19–26; Matthew 5.1–8
John and Charles Wesley (24 May): *also* Ephesians 5.15–20
Lancelot Andrewes (25 Sept): *especially* Isaiah 6.1–8
Martin of Tours (11 Nov): *also* 1 Thessalonians 5.1–11; Matthew 25.34–40
Nicholas (6 Dec): *also* Isaiah 61.1–3; 1 Timothy 6.6–11; Mark 10.13–16
Richard (16 June): *also* John 21.15–19
Swithun (15 July): *also* James 5.7–11, 13–18
Thomas Ken (8 June): *especially* 2 Corinthians 4.1–10 [*or* 1–2, 5–7]; Matthew 24.42–46
Wulfstan (19 Jan): *especially* Matthew 24.42–46

Members of Religious Communities

1 Kings 19.9–18; Proverbs 10.27–end; Song of Solomon 8.6–7; Isaiah 61.10—62.5;
    Hosea 2.14–15, 19–20
Psalms 34.1–8; 112.1–9; 119.57–64; 123; 131
Acts 4.32–35; 2 Corinthians 10.17—11.2; Philippians 3.7–14; 1 John 2.15–17;
    Revelation 19.1, 5–9
Matthew 11.25–end; *or* 19.3–12; *or* 19.23–end; Luke 9.57–end; *or* 12.32–37

Aelred (12 Jan): *also* Ecclesiasticus 15.1–6
Alcuin (20 May): *also* Colossians 3.12–16; John 4.19–24
Antony (17 Jan): *especially* Philippians 3.7–14, *also* Matthew 19.16–26
Bede (25 May): *also* Ecclesiasticus 39.1–10
Benedict (11 July): *also* 1 Corinthians 3.10–11; Luke 18.18–22
Clare (11 Aug): *especially* Song of Solomon 8.6–7
Dominic (8 Aug): *also* Ecclesiasticus 39.1–10
Etheldreda (23 June): *also* Matthew 25.1–13
Francis of Assisi (4 Oct): *also* Galatians 6.14–end; Luke 12.22–34
Hilda (19 Nov): *especially* Isaiah 61.10—62.5
Hildegard (17 Sept): *also* 1 Corinthians 2.9–13; Luke 10.21–24
Julian of Norwich (8 May): *also* 1 Corinthians 13.8–end; Matthew 5.13–16
Vincent de Paul (27 Sept): *also* 1 Corinthians 1.25–end; Matthew 25.34–40

Missionaries

Isaiah 52.7–10; *or* 61.1–3*a*; Ezekiel 34.11–16; Jonah 3.1–5
Psalms 67; *or* 87; *or* 97; *or* 100; *or* 117
Acts 2.14, 22–36; *or* 13.46–49; *or* 16.6–10; *or* 26.19–23; Romans 15.17–21;
    2 Corinthians 5.11—6.2
Matthew 9.35–end; *or* 28.16–end; Mark 16.15–20; Luke 5.1–11; *or* 10.1–9

Aidan (31 Aug): *also* 1 Corinthians 9.16–19
Anskar (3 Feb): *especially* Isaiah 52.7–10; *also* Romans 10.11–15
Chad (2 Mar *or* 26 Oct): *also* 1 Timothy 6.11*b*–16
Columba (9 June): *also* Titus 2.11–end
Cuthbert (20 Mar *or* 4 Sept): *especially* Ezekiel 34.11–16; *also* Matthew 18.12–14
Cyril and Methodius (14 Feb): *especially* Isaiah 52.7–10; *also* Romans 10.11–15
Henry Martyn (19 Oct): *especially* Mark 16.15–end; *also* Isaiah 55.6–11
Ninian (16 Sept): *especially* Acts 13.46–49; Mark 16.15–end
Patrick (17 Mar): *also* Psalm 91.1–4, 13–end; Luke 10.1–12, 17–20
Paulinus (10 Oct); *especially* Matthew 28.16–end
Wilfrid (12 Oct): *especially* Luke 5.1–11; *also* 1 Corinthians 1.18–25
Willibrord (7 Nov): *especially* Isaiah 52.7–10; Matthew 28.16–end

Any Saint

General

Genesis 12.1–4; Proverbs 8.1–11; Micah 6.6–8; Ecclesiasticus 2.7–13 [14–end]
Psalms 32; 33.1–5; 119.1–8; 139.1–4 [5–12]; 145.8–14
Ephesians 3.14–19; *or* 6.11–18; Hebrews 13.7–8, 15–16; James 2.14–17;
    1 John 4.7–16; Revelation 21.[1–4] 5–7
Matthew 19.16–21; *or* 25.1–13; *or* 25.14–30; John 15.1–8; *or* 17.20–end

Christian rulers

1 Samuel 16.1–13*a*; 1 Kings 3.3–14
Psalms 72.1–7; 99
1 Timothy 2.1–6
Mark 10.42–45; Luke 14.27–33

Alfred the Great (26 Oct): *also* 2 Samuel 23.1–5; John 18.33–37
Edward the Confessor (13 Oct): *also* 2 Samuel 23.1–5; 1 John 4.13–16
Margaret of Scotland (16 Nov): *also* Proverbs 31.10–12, 20, 26–end;
    1 Corinthians 12.13—13.3; Matthew 25.34–end

Those working for the poor and underprivileged

Isaiah 58.6–11
Psalms 82; 146.5–10
Hebrews 13.1–3; 1 John 3.14–18
Matthew 5.1–12; *or* 25.31–end

Elizabeth of Hungary (18 Nov): *especially* Matthew 25.31–end; *also* Proverbs 31.10–end
Josephine Butler (30 May): *especially* Isaiah 58.6–11; *also* 1 John 3.18–23; Matthew 9.10–13
William Wilberforce, Olaudah Equiano and Thomas Clarkson (30 July): *also* Job 31.16–23;
    Galatians 3.26–end, 4.6–7; Luke 4.16–21

Men and women of learning

Proverbs 8.22–31; Ecclesiasticus 44.1–15
Psalms 36.5–10; 49.1–4
Philippians 4.7–8
Matthew 13.44–46, 52; John 7.14–18

Those whose holiness was revealed in marriage and family life

Proverbs 31.10–13, 19–20, 30–end; Tobit 8.4–7
Psalms 127; 128
1 Peter 3.1–9
Mark 3.31–end; Luke 10.38–end

Mary Sumner (9 Aug): *also* Hebrews 13.1–5
Monica (27 Aug): *also* Ecclesiasticus 26.1–3, 13–16

¶ Lectionary for Special Occasions

The Guidance of the Holy Spirit

Proverbs 24.3–7; Isaiah 30.15–21; Wisdom 9.13–17
Psalms 25.1–9; 104.26–33; 143.8–10
Acts 15.23–29; Romans 8:22–27; 1 Corinthians 12.4–13
Luke 14.27–33; John 14.23–26; *or* 16.13–15

Rogation Days
(27–29 May in 2019)

Deuteronomy 8.1–10; 1 Kings 8.35–40; Job 28.1–11
Psalms 104.21–30; 107.1–9; 121
Philippians 4.4–7; 2 Thessalonians 3.6–13; 1 John 5.12–15
Matthew 6.1–15; Mark 11.22–24; Luke 11.5–13

Harvest Thanksgiving

Year A	Year B	Year C
Deuteronomy 8.7–18 *or* 28.1–14	Joel 2.21–27	Deuteronomy 26.1–11
Psalm 65	Psalm 126	Psalm 100
2 Corinthians 9.6–end	1 Timothy 2.1–7 *or* 6.6–10	Philippians 4.4–9
Luke 12.16–30 *or* 17.11–19	Matthew 6.25–33	*or* Revelation 14.14–18
		John 6.25–35

Mission and Evangelism

Isaiah 49.1–6; *or* 52.7–10; Micah 4.1–5
Psalms 2; 46; 67
Acts 17.10–end; 2 Corinthians 5.14—6.2; Ephesians 2.13–end
Matthew 5.13–16; *or* 28.16–end; John 17.20–end

The Unity of the Church

Jeremiah 33.6–9*a*; Ezekiel 36.23–28; Zephaniah 3.16–end
Psalms 100; 122; 133
Ephesians 4.1–6; Colossians 3.9–17; 1 John 4.9–15
Matthew 18.19–22; John 11.45–52; *or* 17.11*b*–23

The Peace of the World

Isaiah 9.1–6; *or* 57.15–19; Micah 4.1–5
Psalms 40.14–17; 72.1–7; 85.8–13
Philippians 4.6–9; 1 Timothy 2.1–6; James 3.13–18
Matthew 5.43–end; John 14.23–29; *or* 15.9–17

Social Justice and Responsibility

Isaiah 32.15–end; Amos 5.21–24; *or* 8.4–7; Acts 5.1–11
Psalms 31.21–24; 85.1–7; 146.5–10
Colossians 3.12–15; James 2.1–4
Matthew 5.1–12; *or* 25.31–end; Luke 16.19–end

Ministry, including Ember Days
(See page 7)

Numbers 11.16–17, 24–29; *or* 27.15–end; 1 Samuel 16.1–13*a*; Isaiah 6.1–8;
  or 61.1–3; Jeremiah 1.4–10
Psalms 40.8–13; 84.8–12; 89.19–25; 101.1–5, 7; 122
Acts 20.28–35; 1 Corinthians 3.3–11; Ephesians 4.4–16; Philippians 3.7–14
Luke 4.16–21 *or* 12.35–43 *or* 22.24–27; John 4.31–38 *or* 15.5–17

In Time of Trouble

Genesis 9.8–17; Job 1.13–end; Isaiah 38.6–11
Psalms 86.1–7; 107.4–15; 142.1–7
Romans 3.21–26; Romans 8.18–25; 2 Corinthians 8.1–5, 9
Mark 4.35–end; Luke 12.1–7; John 16.31–end

For the Sovereign

Joshua 1.1–9; Proverbs 8.1–16
Psalms 20; 101; 121
Romans 13.1–10; Revelation 21.22—22.4
Matthew 22.16–22; Luke 22.24–30

The anniversary of HM The Queen's accession is 6 February.

¶ Psalms in the Course of a Month

The following provision may be used for a monthly cycle of psalmody in place of the psalms provided in the tables in this booklet. It is based on the provision in The Book of Common Prayer.

	Morning Prayer	**Evening Prayer**
1	1—5	6—8
2	9—11	12—14
3	15—17	18
4	19—21	22—23
5	24—26	27—29
6	30—31	32—34
7	35—36	37
8	38—40	41—43
9	44—46	47—49
10	50—52	53—55
11	56—58	59—61
12	62—64	65—67
13	68	69—70
14	71—72	73—74
15	75—77	78
16	79—81	82—85
17	86—88	89
18	90—92	93—94
19	95—97	98—101
20	102—103	104
21	105	106
22	107	108—109
23	110—112	113—115
24	116—118	119.1–32
25	119.33–72	119.73–96
26	119.97–144	119.145–176
27	120—125	126—131
28	132—135	136—138
29	139—140	141—143
30	144—146	147—150

In February the psalms are read only to the 28th or 29th day of the month.

In January, March, May, July, August, October and December, all of which have 31 days, the same psalms are read on the last day of the month (being an ordinary weekday) which were read the day before, or else the psalms of the monthly course omitted on one of the Sundays in that month.

Concise Calendar November 2019 – December 2020

Advent 2019 to the eve of Advent 2020: Year A (Daily Eucharistic Lectionary Year 2)

	November 2019					December 2019					January 2020				
Sunday		4bAdv	3bAdv	2bAdv	ChrK	Adv1	Adv2	Adv3	Adv4	Chr1		Chr2	Bapt	Ep2	Ep3
Monday		4	11	18	25	2	9	16	23	30		Epiph	13	20	27
Tuesday		5	12	19	26	3	10	17	24	31		7	14	21	28
Wednesday		6	13	20	27	4	11	18	Chr		1	8	15	22	29
Thursday		7	14	21	28	5	12	19	26		2	9	16	23	30
Friday	AllSs	8	15	22	29	6	13	20	27		3	10	17	24	31
Saturday	2	9	16	23	30	7	14	21	28		4	11	18	25	

	February 2020					March 2020					April 2020				
Sunday		Pres	3bLnt	2bLnt	NbLnt	Lnt1	Lnt2	Lnt3	Lnt4	Lnt5		PmS	Est	Est2	Est3
Monday		3	10	17	24	2	9	16	23	30		6	13	20	27
Tuesday		4	11	18	25	3	10	17	24	31		7	14	21	28
Wednesday		5	12	19	Ash W	4	11	18	Ann		1	8	15	22	29
Thursday		6	13	20	27	5	12	19	26		2	9	16	23	30
Friday		7	14	21	28	6	13	20	27		3	10	17	24	
Saturday	1	8	15	22	29	7	14	21	28		4	11	18	25	

	May 2020					June 2020					July 2020				
Sunday		Est4	Est5	Est6	Est7	Pent	TrS	Tr1	Tr2	Tr3		Tr4	Tr5	Tr6	Tr7
Monday		4	11	18	25	1	8	15	22	29		6	13	20	27
Tuesday		5	12	19	26	2	9	16	23	30		7	14	21	28
Wednesday		6	13	20	27	3	10	17	24		1	8	15	22	29
Thursday		7	14	Ascn	28	4	11	18	25		2	9	16	23	30
Friday	1	8	15	22	29	5	12	19	26		3	10	17	24	31
Saturday	2	9	16	23	30	6	13	20	27		4	11	18	25	

	August 2020						September 2020					October 2020				
Sunday		Tr8	Tr9	Tr10	Tr11	Tr12		Tr13	Tr14	Tr15	Tr16		Tr17	Tr18	Tr19	LstTr
Monday		3	10	17	24	31		7	14	21	28		5	12	19	26
Tuesday		4	11	18	25		1	8	15	22	29		6	13	20	27
Wednesday		5	12	19	26		2	9	16	23	30		7	14	21	28
Thursday		6	13	20	27		3	10	17	24		1	8	15	22	29
Friday		7	14	21	28		4	11	18	25		2	9	16	23	30
Saturday	1	8	15	22	29		5	12	19	26		3	10	17	24	31

	November 2020					December 2020				
Sunday	AllSs	3bAdv	2bAdv	ChrK	Adv1		Adv2	Adv3	Adv4	Chr1
Monday	2	9	16	23	30		7	14	21	28
Tuesday	3	10	17	24		1	8	15	22	29
Wednesday	4	11	18	25		2	9	16	23	30
Thursday	5	12	19	26		3	10	17	24	31
Friday	6	13	20	27		4	11	18	Chr	
Saturday	7	14	21	28		5	12	19	26	

On Sunday 5 January, **Epiphany** may be celebrated, transferred from 6 January.